Jeff's Cold Hard Ice Rulez

1 CLOUDY ICE IS GROSS ICE!

THOSE STANKY 3-MONTH-OLD FUNKY CHUNKS OF PERMAFROST DO NOT BELONG IN A PROPER COCKTAIL. THEY SMELL, LOOK & TASTE FUNNY!

2 AT THE VERY LEAST, BUY A BAG OF ICE

OR HAVE SOMEONE BRING IT! AT LEAST YOU KNOW THE BAGGED STUFF IS CLEAN & CLEAR.

3 PRO MOVE: INVEST IN A CLEAR CUBE MOLD,

WHICH USES GRAVITY TO GIVE YOU THE CLEAREST & PUREST ICE CUBES IMAGINABLE. MOST OF THESE MAKE 4 GIANT CUBES AT A TIME, SO PLAN AHEAD & START MAKING THEM DAYS IN ADVANCE SO YOU HAVE AT LEAST A DOZEN ON HAND FOR THOSE SPECIALTY POURS OF BOURBON, TEQUILA, OR AFTER-DINNER DIGESTIF!

4 INVEST IN A LARGE, INSULATED ICE BUCKET

COMPLETE WITH A BOTTOM STRAINER FOR ALL THAT MELTED RUN OFF. THEY HOLD A LOT AND HOLD IT WELL!

5 FOR GOD'S SAKE, PROVIDE TONGS!

NOTHING WORSE THAN PEOPLE USING THEIR HANDS.

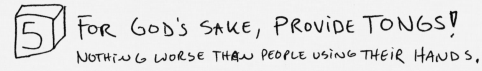

Come On Over

Come On Over

111 FANTASTIC RECIPES FOR THE FAMILY THAT COOKS, EATS, AND LAUGHS TOGETHER

JEFF MAURO

PHOTOGRAPHY BY
KEN GOODMAN

WILLIAM MORROW

An Imprint of HarperCollinsPublishers

Foreword © 2021 Sebastian Maniscalco

Photography by Ken Goodman

Old family photographs courtesy of the author

FIRST EDITION

DESIGNED BY RENATA DE OLIVEIRA

Crown icon by notbad/Shutterstock

Library of Congress Cataloging-in-Publication Data

Names: Mauro, Jeff, author.
Title: Come on over : 110 fantastic recipes for the busiest house on the block /
Jeff Mauro ; photography by Ken Goodman.
Description: First edition. | New York, NY : William Morrow, an imprint of HarperCollins
Publishers, [2021] | Includes index. | Summary: "A personality-filled cookbook for family and
friendly gatherings from celebrity chef Jeff Mauro, co-host of The Kitchen on Food Network"—
Provided by publisher.
Identifiers: LCCN 2020042432 (print) | LCCN 2020042433 (ebook) |
ISBN 9780062997081 (print) | ISBN 9780062997098 (digital edition)
Subjects: LCSH: Cooking. | LCGFT: Cookbooks.
Classification: LCC TX714 .M3766 2021 (print) | LCC TX714 (ebook) |
DDC 641.5-dc23
LC record available at https://lccn.loc.gov/2020042432
LC ebook record available at https://lccn.loc.gov/2020042433

ISBN 978-0-06-299708-1

21 22 23 24 25 WOR 10 9 8 7 6 5 4 3 2 1

THIS BOOK IS DEDICATED TO MY SON LORENZO LUCCA AKA LOLO. REMEMBER, WORK HARD, BE KIND, CREATE CONSTANTLY, AND LAUGH AT LEAST SEVERAL TIMES AN HOUR.

Contents

Foreword

BY SEBASTIAN MANISCALCO

In 2016, while I was performing in my hometown of Chicago, I received a request from my manager that a chef, Jeff Mauro, wanted to come back and say hello. I'd heard of this guy from Chicago who was the self-proclaimed "sandwich king" and told my manager I would love to meet anyone who refers to themselves by my favorite thing to eat. I met Jeff and immediately had a connection with him. He was an Italian guy from Chicago who loved food as much as I loved comedy. Since then, we've remained in contact, and Chef has given me some unbelievable restaurant recommendations—and also introduced me to Sardel cookware. (By the way, I should mention that I think I'm something of a "chef" myself, making all the meals in my house from breakfast to dinner to desserts while my wife chirps over my shoulder, telling me to "give it some more flavor!")

When I heard Jeff was coming out with a cookbook, I couldn't wait to get my hands on it. When I open a cookbook, it usually has a picture, recipe, picture, recipe, and so on and so forth. This cookbook was different. It had humorous anecdotes about the recipes and how they were a part of Jeff's family. I don't know if it's because I'm from Chicago and relate a lot to the food in the book or if it's the way Jeff throws in Chicago references like "frunchroom," but I wanted to make every recipe in the book right then and there. This is the first cookbook I've ever read that shows you exactly how to make a Chicago-style hot dog, and the french fries recipe took me right back to 1983, when I used to stop at Frankly Yours in the northwest suburbs for an order of fries and a Coke.

Jeff has the ability to share his passion for family, cooking, and comedy and wraps it up in a delightful book. When I perform stand-up comedy, I'm looking for the connection to the audience to take them on a journey of relatable experiences, and Jeff does the exact same thing, only through food. He not only gives you the history of a dish but also brings it to life with humor and heart. Oh, and one more thing, Jeff—I want a *sangwheeech* the next time I see you!

—SEBASTIAN MANISCALCO

Introduction

Come on over . . .

Madone, did I love hearing my mother utter those words into the handset of our wall-mounted landline phone with the obscenely long cord. You see, these were the pre-cordless phone days, and my mother had customized the phone with an upgraded cord that was at least 120 nautical feet long. She could easily gab with her lady friends from any room on the first floor, and at any given time there would be two or three Mauro children tangled up in its wake. The Mauro kids didn't care. When my mom spoke that phrase into that phone, we knew two things would happen: (1) people were coming over, and (2) *We. Were. Going. To. Eat.*

I learned from a young age that company coming over meant the presence of my two favorite things: family and food. You see, I come from a very large and very hungry family. My mother has four siblings, and they all had four children (except my uncle Neil—he had three wonderful daughters . . . slacker). So, if you carry the one and do some algebraic math, you figure out *real* quick that I have fifteen first cousins, who now have dozens of kids as well. And that's just on my mother's side! We're like Chicago's Italian American Mogwai, except if you feed us after midnight we only grow chubbier. Additionally, we all live within a couple of miles of one another. Add to this my dad's two sisters, Aunt Fran and Aunt Catherine, my grandma, my great-aunts, the second, third, and fourth cousins, the family friends you *call* your cousins but really aren't your cousins, Dad's buddies, and Mom's girlfriends (all named Barb or Linda) and you can start to deduce that at my house the company was constant, the fun was endless, and the food was plentiful.

Uncle Dave is popping in for some coffee? My mom usually baked her homemade coffee cake, laden with teeth-zingingly sugary icing and paired with endless pots of black tar coffee. Hosting little sister Emily's tenth birthday party or Dana's confirmation celebration? It was an absolute feast. Platters of meatballs and mostaccioli, gallons of charred burgers and jumbo hot dogs, vats of oily sausage and peppers, simple yet succulent pork roast swimming in juicy drippings, fire-engine-red meat loaf, often mediocre cakes, boxes of cannoli, Aunt Jae's chocolate chip cookies . . . It was always damn exciting to have so many food options while being surrounded by gaggles of laughs and loved ones. My cousins and I had so much fun sequestered in the basement, wrestling, yelling, and putting on stupid variety shows.

But ya know what I loved more than all that family action? Being called up for dinner.

For forty years I've observed and absorbed so much from the matriarchs in my life: my mom, Grandma Kay, Aunt Jae, Aunt Phil, Aunt Fran, and Aunt Catherine. Each host had her own methodology, her own idiosyncrasies, her own signature flavor. I gleaned as much as I could while piling food on plate after plate and watching people around a table eat, drink, and laugh. Now, as a bona fide card-carrying adult, living in my own home complete with my own kitchen and my very own family, I've become quite the host myself. We have a house perfect for entertaining, and we do so very, very often. Sarah, my partner and wife for twenty years, will usually start things off by saying, "Should we have people over?" "Should we host Easter?" "What do you think? Just have people over here on Saturday? We can make pizza. Keep it simple, though . . ."

But it's never quite so simple, is it? The shopping, prepping, setting up, cooking, and of course, the dreaded cleaning. I'm not saying I'm here to make everything simple. That's near impossible. But I definitely can help with tried-and-true recipes that have satisfied my family for generations, as well as modern and whimsical twists on some of my favorites that I've developed over my career. I also have plenty of time-honored tips that will help ease your pain. Here is a list of *Come On Over* commandments that I've compiled over the years:

THE TEN *COME ON OVER* COMMANDMENTS

1. Though it's never truly simple, you should keep it as simple as possible.
2. You can never overprepare.
3. One to *zero* apps. Keep your guests *hungry* to make dinner the star.
4. You can never have too much ice.
5. Nothing is wrong with quality disposables.
6. People will ask, "What should I bring?" When in doubt . . . ice and booze.
7. Having a theme makes menu planning easier.
8. Stay in your wheelhouse, and cook what you know.
9. Enjoy the meal . . . if you can. Too often the cook doesn't sit down and dine with the guests. I'm very guilty of this, as are my wife, mother, aunts, cousins, everyone. Make sure you take a breath, make a plate, and join the family for a well-deserved meal.
10. *It's always worth it!*

Come on, you know I'm right. It's always worth it! Sure, cleanup is indeed *a bitch*, and things tend to get hectic when guests start to arrive, but whether you're hosting Christmas Eve, July 4th, Uncle Neil's seventieth birthday, or just some coffee with your old man, there's always plenty of joy to be found in a gathering. Some welcome the craziness of those first moments when everyone shows up and there's a cacophony of "Where should I put this giant dish full of many things?" and "Where do the coats go?" and "You got any Pinot Grigio?" Many love the middle piece, the actual meat of the party when drinks are flowing and the playlist is actually playing. Quite a few are in it for the end, when all is tidy, the leftovers are wrapped, and you can enjoy your first peaceful beverage and bask in the silent afterglow. Me, I'm a sucker for those tasty ten minutes before the brood floods in, when you and your loved one can pour a glass of chewy red or crack open a hazy IPA and enjoy that first swipe of hummus or the inaugural shard from a fresh wedge of crunchy Parm.

It's *those* personal magical moments that keep the host hosting, the guests gathering, and the families fed, full, and together. In a world of screen-dominated dinners, it's nice to just say, screw it, "We'll host . . . Come on over!" So, fire up the grill, shuffle that playlist, pop a bottle, and let's break some bread.

Now the only question is . . . what should we make?

SALUT!

Pinot G and JoJo doing their famous and dangerous double "up"

1

EARLY BIRD GETS THE BRUNCH

I rarely eat breakfast. I'm a big intermittent faster and believe that it has contributed to my overall weight loss and health. I won't bore you with the finer points (I'll save that for a healthy-themed tome), but for me it means that I usually eat only lunch and dinner and stop eating immediately after dinner, around 5:30 PM. But because I still and always will adore breakfast meats, breakfast breads, and eggs, I often eat breakfast for lunch. Come to the Mauro house on any given weekday around 1:00 PM and there will be plenty of bacon and egg cookery going on. Little did I know that this is an actual *thing* that young adults do for fun! It's called *brunch*, and it's literally eating both breakfast foods and lunch foods for lunch while tossing back twelve to fifteen bottom-shelf mimosas and having lots of laughs and TikTok-ing on the worldwide internet.

Gus's Kitchen Sink Frittata

MAKES 4 TO 6 SERVINGS

My father, Gus, did very little cooking when I was growing up. He essentially made three things: milkshakes, Atomic Hash Browns (page 9), and this frittata. He reserved the frittata for special occasions—usually Easter and Christmas morning after mass. To put it mildly, the making of this frittata was an immense production involving cutting boards, pan, spatulas, and puddles of albumin strewn about the kitchen. Ingredient-wise, nothing was off limits. Twenty-four large eggs, a pound of cubed cheese, cold cuts, Italian sausage, leftover chicken Vesuvio from the pizza joint—each made an appearance at some point.

Once the eggs were cooked somewhat firm, it was time for the flip. He would invert a large dinner plate over the somewhat-runny frittata, then precariously flip it onto said dinner plate. We would watch from afar, like front-row splash-zone spectators at Sea World, nervous to get splashed but also kind of hoping to get splashed. We'd gasp as it slid around the dinner plate, dripping egg down to the floor. But like a true maestro, Gus always guided the frittata home by carefully sliding it back in the pan, where it would finish cooking. Sure, the kitchen looked like an egg-based crime scene, but there was also a pretty darn great frittata, evenly "fried" on both sides.

Looking back, Gus's culinary method of the frittata flip was totally preposterous yet 100 percent *Gus*: how to get successfully from point A to point B in the most complicated way possible.

JEFFREY MICHAEL MAURO'S PROFESSIONAL TIP: *I've slightly updated the methodology with a cleaner and much easier method of popping the frittata under the broiler to finish. As far as the ingredients, go to town with whatever meat, cheese, or veg you have. Also, if you're feeling frisky, by all means, don't fear the flip . . . in honor of Gus.*

8 slices bacon, cut into ¼-inch pieces
½ pound bulk hot Italian sausage
12 large eggs
3 tablespoons half-and-half
1 cup grated Asiago (about 4 ounces)
1 cup grated provolone (about 4 ounces)
Kosher salt and freshly ground
    black pepper

1. Adjust an oven rack to the middle position and preheat the oven to broil.

2. Place the bacon in an ovenproof 12-inch nonstick skillet set over medium heat and cook until just crisp, 4 to 5 minutes. Set aside on a paper towel–lined plate.

3. Add the sausage to the pan and cook until well browned, breaking it up as it cooks, 10 to 12 minutes. Add the sausage to the bacon, leaving the pork fat in the skillet.

4. In a medium bowl, whisk the eggs and half-and-half until smooth. Add the egg mixture to the skillet with the pork fat and set it over medium heat. Using a rubber spatula, stir the eggs until they start to set, scraping and tilting the pan to fill any gaps with the loose mixture.

Cook until the bottom is set and the top is still wet and glistening, 2 to 3 minutes. Scatter the cooked meats and cheeses evenly over the frittata and season with salt and pepper to taste. Use the spatula to press the ingredients into the eggs.

5. Place the skillet in the oven and broil until lightly golden on top and puffed up, 2 to 4 minutes. Let the frittata rest for about 5 minutes before slicing.

6. Slide the frittata onto a cutting board and cut into wedges. Season with more salt and pepper if desired.

This is the overspiced hue you are looking for. Red like a warning sign . . . just like Gus makes 'em.

Gus's Atomic Hash Browns

MAKES 4 TO 6 SERVINGS

As chubby little ones, the Mauro kids would always be served these hash browns with Gus's Kitchen Sink Frittata (page 6). It's the perfect pairing: crispy and intensely spiced hash browns with the indulgent frittata. The key to making this dish sing is adding way more spices, salt, and pepper than you would think is appropriate. Your eyes should taste it before your tongue. That too is 100 percent Gus: Anything worth doing is worth overdoing.

JEFF'S TIP: *Seriously, don't be afraid to bump up the heat and salt on these, and always, no matter what, make them extra crispy. I love crisping up only one side of these hash browns. The contrast of ultra-oily, crispy potatoes with creamy, warm, untouched potatoes is diner magic.*

2 pounds russet potatoes, peeled, coarsely grated on a box grater, and squeezed dry in a kitchen towel
1 teaspoon granulated garlic
1 teaspoon smoked paprika
¼ to ½ teaspoon cayenne pepper
1 teaspoon kosher salt
½ teaspoon freshly ground black pepper
2 tablespoons unsalted butter
2 tablespoons olive oil

1. Toss the potatoes, granulated garlic, paprika, cayenne, salt, and pepper in a large bowl.

2. Melt the butter and oil together in a large nonstick skillet over medium heat, then add the potatoes, pressing them down with a spatula. Cook until crisp and golden brown on one side, 5 to 7 minutes, or until you start to see the golden brown "creep" up the edges. To take the browns even further, cook 3 to 5 minutes more, peeking under the potatoes to ensure that an extra-crispy texture is achieved.

3. Place a lightweight cutting board over the skillet and carefully flip so that the crispy side is on top. Cut into wedges to serve.

Grapevine, Kentucky, Buttermilk Biscuits

MAKES 4 TO 6 SERVINGS

I fell in love with these biscuits at the same time I fell in love with Sarah. We were barely twenty-one, both still living at home with our folks, and spent many an evening crashing at each other's homes—sleeping in "separate bedrooms," of course. We would often go out *hard* on Saturday nights, hitting up Chicago's finest clubs: Jilly's Retro, Red No. 5, Funk.

Sleeping over at Sarah's house was the best because every Sunday morning I would wake to the smell of bacon sizzling, pork chops frying, and biscuits baking. Bluegrass would be playing on the system, and maybe Uncle Frank was over, or Uncle Garland, or Uncle Harvey, or Aunt Margaret. Nothing helped erase the hangover from the previous evening like lively conversation in a *thicc*-as-sorghum eastern Kentucky drawl paired with a side of a warm biscuit swimming in homemade sausage gravy and fried pig meat. It was my first taste of the Appalachian culture, which I quickly discovered wasn't too far from my Italian-American upbringing. Accents, gallons of food, and plenty of laughs and ball busting. I was quickly hooked.

Sarah Edith Mauro (née Jones) is a true city girl, born and raised in Chicago proper. Her parents, though—Mrs. Marjorie Alice Ross Jones and Mr. James Paul Jones—were born and raised in the great state of Kentucky. Alice is from a holler in Grapevine, Kentucky (Perry County), and is one of seventeen children. My father-in-law, Paul, is from the slightly more bucolic Kentucky town of Barbourville and once lost a trigger finger playing the "knife game" with his friend Bo McCoury.* Their stories are just as authentic as their food, especially Alice's Sunday breakfast. *Especially* these biscuits.

As of 2021, Sarah and I have been together for twenty-one years. My mother-in-law, Alice, has been making these biscuits in the same cast-iron skillet for three times that long, following her mother before her, who made them in the same damn skillet.

LI'L JEFFIE'S TIP: *The key is the flour; Alice gets hers from Kentucky. Look for White Lily or Hudson Cream self-rising flour. It's legit.*

4 cups self-rising flour, plus more for dusting

8 tablespoons (1 stick) salted butter, cut into 1-inch slices, plus more for serving

2 to 3 cups cold buttermilk

1 tablespoon vegetable oil

3 tablespoons salted butter, melted

Honey, for serving

Sausage Gravy (page 23), for serving

continues

---

* My father-in-law actually lost two fingers. Bo McCoury,** who was playing alongside Paul, got spooked and threw both fingers into the "crick." One finger, the much-maligned middle finger, was promptly recovered and reattached by one of Kentucky's finest finger doctors. The other one? Lost to the waters. This story has passed through the grapevine enough to become official lore. This is how the story lives in my mind—and it's a perfect portrait of Paul. I do not want to seek out the actual story if it indeed differs. I don't care. I want it to last forever and ever and ever. I can't help but run through the fantastical scenario in my mind every time I take a fleeting glance at my father-in-law's missing finger.

** Not his actual name. I made it up. Don't want to ask Paul for clarification and facts because of the above . . .

1. Preheat the oven to 425°F. Place a heavy 12-inch cast-iron skillet in the oven to preheat. Chill a large bowl, pastry cutter, the flour, and the sliced butter in the freezer for 15 minutes before assembling the biscuits.

2. Add the flour to the chilled bowl. Working quickly, cut the cold butter slices into the flour using the chilled pastry cutter (or your fingers). The goal is to form pea-size balls of butter. In 10 to 12 batches, stir in the buttermilk until the dough is cohesive and moist.

3. Turn out the dough onto a floured surface and lightly press into a 1-inch-thick round.

Using a 4-inch biscuit cutter or the business end of a dry measuring cup, cut out 6 to 8 biscuits. Repress the scraps and cut out another biscuit or two.

4. Remove the skillet from the oven and add the oil. Crowd the biscuits in the skillet so that they are touching one another, brush with the melted butter, and bake until golden brown, 20 to 25 minutes. Let them cool for a couple of minutes and then turn them out upside down on a cutting board. Serve with plenty of salted butter, honey, and a big ol' boat of gravy!

Vanilla-Lemon Buttermilk Pancakes with Chantilly Cream

MAKES 8 LARGE PANCAKES

Like any young child on this planet Earth, Lorenzo *loves* pancakes. I do have to confess, though, that we often resort to the "just add water" box mix. Sometimes you just don't have no time. These are totally worth it, especially on a Sunday morning while *Breakfast with the Beatles* is playing in the background, the coffee is brewing, and, hopefully, the sun is streaming through the kitchen window. Oh yeah . . . crispy bacon is a must. Please serve this with crispy bacon. If you can't tell already, the Mauros love crispy. Sure, you can drown this in good maple syrup, but I prefer a generous dollop of fresh Chantilly cream, which helps amplify the vanilla and bright lemon flavors.

JEFF'S TIDBIT OF THE DAY: *Make a double batch for a crowd or, if cooking for future you, individually wrap each leftover pancake in plastic wrap and freeze. When it's a hectic weekday morning and you want something homemade in your little one's tum-tum, take out a couple pancakes, unwrap, and slide into your toaster on medium-low to simultaneously defrost, reheat, and lightly crisp to the ideal pancake texture.*

TWO-TIPS TUESDAY: *The Mauro house is obsessed with our square flat-bottomed, shallow-walled nonstick skillet. I realize that's a lot of descriptors, but this is the perfect pancake pan. It fits 4 pancakes (or grilled cheese sandwiches or French toast slices or fried eggs) at once and the low walls make it easy for a spatula to get up in there and flip whatever is on the pan. It's the most underrated pan in the world. We go through one of these a year and usually just order the OXO one off Amazon. Reminder: If you use your nonstick pans a lot, be sure get rid of them once they start showing wear and tear!*

CHANTILLY CREAM

1 cup heavy (whipping) cream
1 tablespoon vanilla bean paste or 1 teaspoon pure vanilla extract
3 tablespoons confectioners' sugar

PANCAKES

2 cups all-purpose flour
2 tablespoons granulated sugar
½ teaspoon kosher salt
½ teaspoon baking soda
1 teaspoon baking powder
2 cups buttermilk
¼ cup sour cream
2 large eggs
3 tablespoons unsalted butter, melted and cooled
1½ teaspoons vanilla bean paste or pure vanilla extract
1 tablespoon lemon zest, plus 1 teaspoon for serving
2 tablespoons fresh lemon juice
2 teaspoons vegetable oil
½ cup fresh blueberries, for serving

1. To make the Chantilly cream, combine the cream, vanilla bean paste, and confectioners' sugar in a large cold bowl. Using a hand mixer,

continues

whip on medium speed until medium peaks form, 5 to 7 minutes. Cover with plastic wrap and refrigerate until serving.

2. To make the pancakes, whisk the flour, sugar, salt, baking soda, and baking powder in a large bowl. Whisk the buttermilk, sour cream, eggs, butter, vanilla bean paste, 1 tablespoon lemon zest, and the lemon juice in a medium bowl. Pour the wet mixture into the dry mixture and gently mix with a spatula until just combined but still lumpy. Do not overmix.

3. Preheat the oven to 200°F and place a wire rack on a rimmed sheet pan.

4. Heat 1 teaspoon of the oil in a square flat-bottomed nonstick griddle pan or nonstick skillet over medium heat. Working in batches, ladle ¼ cup of the batter per pancake onto the griddle. Cook the pancakes for 3 to 5 minutes, until the bottom is golden and the top starts to bubble. Flip and cook for another 3 to 5 minutes. Set the cooked pancake on the prepared rack in the oven to keep warm. Repeat to cook more pancakes to your family's desire. Trust me, if you don't cook enough, you'll hear about it!

5. Top the pancakes with fresh blueberries and the remaining lemon zest and serve with Chantilly cream.

Four Ways to the Perfect Egg

Don't ever underestimate the importance and nuances of egg cookery. There may be at least thirty-two hundred ways to cook an egg correctly, but these methods are how I do it since they've always worked for me at home. I purposefully omit hard-boiled eggs in my concept of "perfect" eggs because they lie at no. 2 on my no-no list, right under cottage cheese and just above mayo-based tuna fish salad.

Full disclosure: This recipe took the longest to shoot photos of, not because of the recipes or food styling but because of my terrible habit of misspelling and rushing through things. The brilliant "handwriting on parchment" idea was Lisa's. Too bad she didn't realize whom she was deeling [*sic*] with.

It took me three tries to get everything spelled right.

Sunny Side Up

MAKES 2 SERVINGS

1 teaspoon olive oil
2 large eggs
Kosher salt
Freshly ground black pepper

1. Set a 10- or 12-inch nonstick skillet (whichever has a lid!) over medium-low heat. Add the oil and swirl around to coat the skillet.
2. Crack the eggs into a small bowl and then gently slide from the bowl onto the skillet. Season with salt and pepper.
3. Cook until the bottom of the white is set, then, using the corner of a thin spatula, poke little slits in the egg white surrounding the yolk to help the white "drain down" and make contact with the pan, thus cooking it evenly. Cover and cook for 1 to 2 minutes, until the white is totally set but the yolk still runny.
4. It's easiest to slide the eggs right onto a plate or into one's mouthal area.

Fried

MAKES 2 SERVINGS

½ tablespoon unsalted butter
2 large eggs

In a 10-inch nonstick skillet over medium-low heat, melt the butter until the foaming subsides, about 2 minutes. Crack the eggs into a small bowl and then gently slide from the bowl onto the skillet. Cook for 2 to 3 minutes, or until the egg white just starts to solidify, and flip. Cook for 1 minute more for over easy or 2 to 3 minutes for over medium.

Scrambled

MAKES 2 SERVINGS

2 large eggs
½ teaspoon kosher salt
2 tablespoons unsalted butter

1. In a small bowl, whisk the eggs and salt until the color is a smooth yellow, with no streaks of white.
2. Set a 10- or 12-inch nonstick skillet over medium-low heat (and I mean medium-low— we don't want color on these bad boys). Melt 1 tablespoon of the butter in the pan and swirl it around to get an even coating.
3. Pour the egg mixture into the pan and let it sit for about 45 seconds. Using a rubber spatula, start moving the eggs around. You'll see the eggs on the bottom start to set.
4. Cook for 4 to 5 minutes while continuing to move the eggs around gently, creating little egg pillows. At this point, the eggs should be about 90 percent set. Turn off the heat and add the remaining 1 tablespoon butter. Stir into the eggs to create the creamiest scrambled eggs you've ever had!

Poached

MAKES 1 SERVING

1 teaspoon white vinegar
1 large egg

1. Fill a low-sided saucepan or high-sided skillet with water to about 2 inches from the top. Bring to a simmer over medium-low heat. Add the vinegar.
2. Crack the egg into a ladle. Slowly lower the egg into the simmering water, letting the hot water fill the ladle but not releasing the egg into the water. Let it sit like that for 15 to 20 seconds to start cooking the egg white, then release the egg into the water. Cook for about 3 minutes, until the egg white is set and the yolk is still soft and runny. Use a slotted spoon to remove the egg to a plate lined with paper towels.

Mauro Method Bacon— the Perfect and Friendliest Way to Bacon

MAKES 6 SERVINGS

The Mauro Method ensures a crisp cook and easy cleanup with no stovetop splatter. Because you overlap parchment around the perimeter of a sheet pan, the fat will render and pool around the bacon just like in a frying pan and will fry the bacon to a perfect crisp. The parchment barrier makes it so the fat will not come in contact with the metal, creating a mess or burning the fat. When the grease is cool, just toss the parchment in the garbage, or, better yet, reserve all that fabulous fat! No draining or scrubbing messy bacon splatter off your stovetop and backsplash. Save yourself time and cleaning supplies. Trust in the Method.

12 slices bacon, not too thick! (We love Oscar Mayer for its balance of fat, sweet, and salt)

1. Preheat the oven to 375°F. Line a rimmed sheet pan with parchment paper, overlapping each side by 1 to 2 inches. Place the bacon in a single layer on the pan and bake, rotating after 8 minutes, until the bacon reaches your desired crispiness, 15 to 20 minutes. Remove the bacon and let drain on a paper towel–lined plate.

2. While the fat is still in liquid form, pour it into an airtight container and store in the fridge for future use for up to 2 weeks. Or for easy cleanup, set the tray aside to cool and carefully toss the parchment with the solidified fat directly in the garbage.

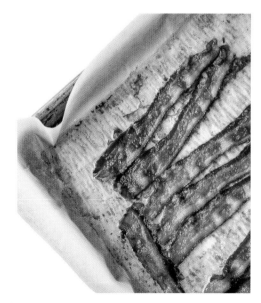

It's all about the parchment overhang!

Sausage, Egg, and Cheese Breakfast Sandos

MAKES 8 BREAKFAST SANDOS

Not sure who invented the sausage, egg, and cheese breakfast sandwich, but I'm pretty sure it was a prehistoric Neanderthal caveperson, right after they discovered fire, chickens, wheat, and cows. FACTS.

MR. MAURO'S TIMESAVING TIP: *These freeze very well and reheat perfectly in the microwave. Grab, nuke, and go. By the time you get to the family truckster or train and unwrap, you'll swear you just went through the drive-thru.*

One 14-ounce tube packaged pork breakfast sausage, cut into eight 1-inch patties
12 large eggs
3 tablespoons half-and-half
1½ teaspoons sea salt
½ teaspoon freshly ground black pepper
4 ounces aged Cheddar, cut into ¼-inch dice
8 English muffins, cut in half and lightly toasted

1. Adjust an oven rack to the middle position and preheat the oven to broil.
2. Set a 12-inch nonstick skillet over medium heat. Add the sausage slices and press them down until "smashed," about ¾ inch thick. Cook 5 minutes on each side, until slightly charred and no longer pink in the middle. Remove the patties and drain on a paper towel–lined plate. Reserve the fat in the skillet.
3. Whisk the eggs, half-and-half, salt, and pepper in a large bowl. Still on medium heat, add the egg mixture to the fat in the skillet and stir the eggs using a rubber spatula, scraping and tilting the pan until large curds form, 2 to 4 minutes. The egg mixture should still be slightly wet. Sprinkle the cheese evenly over the eggs.
4. Finish the eggs in the oven until they are a spotty brown and puffed up, 2 to 4 minutes. Using a pastry round or circular cookie cutter, cut into rounds the same size as the English muffin, about 3 to 4 inches.
5. Build the sandwiches with rounds of frittata (and any extra shards of frittata for extra protein) and sausage patties between English muffin halves. Serve immediately or, for later use, wrap in parchment, then tightly in plastic wrap, and freeze. For a weekly grab-and-go breakfast, defrost overnight, *take off the plastic* (leave on the parchment), and microwave until hot, 1 minute. You can also just pop the frozen sandwich in the microwave for 1 to 2 minutes.

Sausage Gravy

MAKES 4 TO 6 SERVINGS

This gravy must be made when making the Grapevine, Kentucky, Buttermilk Biscuits (page 10). There really is no choice. So make sure you have a roll of fresh breakfast sausage—Jimmy Dean or Tennessee Pride will really do the trick. Do not substitute sausage links. It just ain't the same . . .

One 14-ounce tube packaged breakfast
    sausage, cut into eight ¾-inch slices
1 tablespoon unsalted butter
2 tablespoons all-purpose flour
1 cup whole milk
Kosher salt and freshly ground black pepper

1. Set a 12-inch skillet over medium heat and add the sliced sausage. Brown it until crisp and fairly dark on both sides, 5 to 7 minutes per side or until an internal temperature of 165°F is reached. Reserve the fat in the pan and set aside the sausage on a paper towel–lined plate for the main event.

2. Add the butter to the reserved fat and melt it over medium heat. Add the flour and cook, whisking constantly until it's blond and has a nutty aroma, 2 to 3 minutes. Slowly whisk in the milk, then season with salt and pepper. Simmer until thickened, 3 to 5 minutes.

3. Break two of the sausage patties into small pieces and add them to the gravy for that down-home vibe. Serve up the remaining sausage patties with a gravy boat filled to the brim and *pour gravy over everything you encounter this morning.*

Beggin' for a biscuit . . .

Marjorie Alice Ross Jones's Fried Pork Chops . . . for Breakfast

MAKES 4 TO 6 SERVINGS

The first time I was served a fried pork chop for breakfast I was actually taken aback. I mean, who serves fried pork chops alongside fried pork sausage and crispy pork bacon? A true hero does, that's who.

4 boneless pork loin chops (24 to 32 ounces total), pounded to about ½ inch thickness
Kosher salt and freshly ground black pepper
2 tablespoons vegetable oil
1 cup self-rising flour

1. Season the chops liberally with salt and pepper. If you remember and have the time, place them on a sheet pan and refrigerate uncovered overnight to dry-brine. Try not to skip this step. This is my personal addition to the recipe and it really makes for more tender and juicier chops.

2. To cook, set a large skillet over medium heat and add the oil.

3. Spread the flour on a large plate and add 1 teaspoon kosher salt and ½ teaspoon freshly ground black pepper. Dredge each chop in the flour and shake off the excess.

4. Gently place the pork chops into the hot oil and fry for 4 to 5 minutes on each side, until golden brown.

5. Serve immediately with biscuits and gravy and sausage and bacon and eggs and hot coffee and butter and honey and more biscuits.

These you can totally eat with your hand, holding on to that little bone.

Cranberry-Walnut Irish Soda Bread Muffins with Whipped Maple-Cinnamon Cream Cheese

MAKES 12 MUFFINS

My parents went on one big vacation a year, without the four children. It was usually somewhere totally eighties, like Acapulco or Key West. They would leave us in the care of my dad's sisters, Aunt Fran and Aunt Catherine, who were the best—and our most requested—sitters. But every so often, they weren't available, so they would have to call in the reserve babysitter. This was a young twenty-something named Kathy Fiorito. She somehow managed to keep us all on somewhat of a schedule while successfully preventing us from destroying our home or one another, all the while being that cool and fun young babysitter you read about in Judy Blume novels.

It was like our own little vacation. Rules were looser, pizza was delivered more frequently, and Kathy often made us Irish soda bread, which was odd considering she was from an Italian-American household and cooking for a bunch of Italian-American children. Maybe it was because her boyfriend was Irish, or my parents' vacation usually fell during the week of St. Paddy's Day, or maybe she was half Irish, which was rare yet not unheard of in our world. Regardless, I remember a loaf of somehow moist yet crumbly soda bread sitting on the stove, just waiting to be thoroughly smeared with a big ol' hunk of cream cheese.

DR. MAURO'S SODA BREAD TIP OF THE DAY: *If you don't have cream cheese, salted butter is a damn fine substitute.*

Nonstick cooking spray
½ cup dried cranberries
1 cup Guinness Extra Stout
2¼ cups all-purpose flour
⅓ cup granulated sugar
2 teaspoons baking powder
¼ teaspoon baking soda
½ teaspoon kosher salt
1 large egg
1 cup buttermilk
6 tablespoons unsalted butter, melted
½ cup chopped walnuts
Flaky sea salt, for garnish
Demerara sugar, for garnish
1 recipe Whipped Maple-Cinnamon Cream Cheese (recipe follows), full-fat cream cheese, or softened butter, for serving

1. Preheat the oven to 400°F. Spray a 12-muffin tin liberally with nonstick cooking spray.

2. Combine the cranberries and Guinness in a small microwave-safe bowl. Microwave on high for 45 seconds, then set aside to steep and cool, which will saturate those cranberries with all that lovely beer flavor. Strain and set aside.

3. Combine the flour, sugar, baking powder, baking soda, and salt in a large bowl. Whisk the egg, buttermilk, and butter in a medium bowl.

Add the wet mixture to the dry and stir until just mixed. Do not overmix—you just want all the dry ingredients hydrated. Gently fold in the cranberries and walnuts.

4. Fill each muffin well about three-quarters full. Top each with a pinch of flaky sea salt and demerara sugar. Bake for 18 to 25 minutes, until a toothpick or cake tester comes out clean.

5. Let cool for 5 minutes in the pan, then quickly and carefully remove the muffins from the tin. Finish cooling on a wire rack. Keep the muffins for up to 2 days in an airtight container at room temperature. To properly reinvigorate, refresh in a 400°F oven or toaster oven for 5 minutes.

6. Serve with Whipped Maple-Cinnamon Cream Cheese, cream cheese, or butter.

Whipped Maple-Cinnamon Cream Cheese

Use this magical blend on everything!

MAKES ABOUT 1 CUP

One 8-ounce package full-fat cream cheese, at room temperature
¼ cup pure maple syrup
1 teaspoon ground cinnamon
1 teaspoon kosher salt

1. In a large bowl, use a hand mixer on medium-high speed to whip the cream cheese, maple syrup, cinnamon, and salt until smooth.

2. Store in an airtight container in the fridge for up to 2 weeks.

That ain't vanilla
ice cream. That's
scoops of salted
butter.

Charred Corn Cakes with Fresno Syrup

MAKES 12 MEDIUM CAKES, TO SERVE 4 TO 6

Many consider the West Loop to be Chicago's culinary epicenter. Before everyone had a restaurant in the West Loop, there was a lone wolf, Wishbone, which was right down the block from Harpo Studios and not far from my dad's real estate office on Taylor Street. It had a very quirky vibe, with an innovative menu heavy on the creole, Cajun, and brunch dishes.

On the menu was a corn cake dish that I loved so much. The cakes were stacked high and served with sweet and spicy syrup, and, dare I say, they were somewhat sophisticated for a chubby twelve-year-old.

FRESNO MAPLE SYRUP

1 Fresno chile, cored, seeded, and thinly sliced
1 cup pure maple syrup

CHARRED CORN CAKES

4 tablespoons vegetable oil
2 cups fresh corn kernels (from about 4 ears)
  or one 12-ounce bag frozen corn kernels
1 cup all-purpose flour
1 cup fine ground cornmeal
2 teaspoons sugar
2 teaspoons baking powder
1 teaspoon kosher salt
1¼ cups milk
6 tablespoons (¾ stick) unsalted butter,
  melted
1 large egg, whisked
2 green onions, thinly sliced on the bias, plus
  more for garnish

1. To make the peppery syrup, combine the Fresno chile and maple syrup in a medium saucepan over medium-low heat and bring to a simmer. Reduce the heat to low and let steep for about 20 minutes. When ready to serve, remove the chile pieces and place the syrup in a gravy boat. It's not just for gravy.

2. To make the corn cakes, set a 12-inch skillet over medium-high heat. Add 1 tablespoon of the oil and the corn and sauté for 4 to 5 minutes, until the corn is nicely charred. Remove from the skillet and transfer to a large plate to cool.

3. Combine the flour, cornmeal, sugar, baking powder, salt, and 1 cup of the charred corn (reserve the rest for garnish). Add the milk, 2 tablespoons of the melted butter, the egg, and the green onions and mix until fully combined.

4. Heat 1 tablespoon of the oil in a square flat-bottomed nonstick griddle pan (not a grill pan) over medium heat. Working in batches, ladle ¼ cup of the batter per corn cake onto the griddle. Cook until fluffy and golden brown, 2 to 3 minutes per side. Repeat with the remaining batter, adding in another tablespoon of oil before each batch.

5. Plate the corn cakes and top with dollops of the remaining butter, a nice drizzle of Fresno maple syrup, additional green onion slices, and the remaining charred corn.

One of my
favorite bands,
Dr. Dog!

2

HEY, BRO, WE'RE WATCHING THE GAME . . .
PICK UP SOME ICE ON THE WAY

I am admittedly the least informed sports fan in my personal universe. When I find myself in a sports-focused conversation I do one of two things: pretend *hard* or just admit jokingly that I was busy during that sporting match watching trashy reality programming on Bravo or E!.

The only sports team I actively watch is the Chicago Bears. My attention span can easily handle one game a week for sixteen weeks. Anything beyond that is a chore, and I'd rather be cooking, serving, and eating. Therefore, I *love* hosting any and all sporting events. I get to devote *all* my attention to putting out a fantastic spread of my guilty-pleasure foods. The fried, the meaty, the cheesy, the bready . . . cold beer, great company. This chapter hits all the bases and knocks it out of the park while dunking footballs of flavor into the end zone of your friends' and family's taste buds and tummies. Nothin' but net.

Candied Bacon

MAKES 12 TO 14 SLICES

This method has been perfected for many years. The key is good, fatty bacon. And patience. Also timing: You need to pull it at the right moment, when amber meets mahogany. This is the bacon that puts the *B* in my BLT Sliders (page 34).

Nonstick cooking spray
2 cups unpacked light brown sugar
12 to 14 slices medium-cut applewood smoked
    bacon (the fattier the better)

1. Preheat the oven to 275°F. Line a rimmed sheet pan with foil, spray it with nonstick cooking spray, and set a wire rack on the pan. Spray a second wire rack and set aside.

2. Place the brown sugar in a pie dish. Gently press each slice of bacon into the sugar until coated (there can be patches of uncoated bacon). Work quickly, as the brown sugar can compromise the moisture of the bacon and impede caramelization. Set the bacon on the prepared rack set in the sheet pan as you work.

3. Bake until super crispy and golden, rotating the sheet pan midway through cooking, 50 to 60 minutes total depending on your oven and the thickness of the bacon.

4. Remove the bacon right away to the other prepared wire rack to keep it from sticking. Cool for 30 minutes, until peak crispness is achieved. Take a brittle bite and realize quickly that this here bite of candied bacon is one of the greatest bites you've taken. Maybe not *ever*, maybe not even this year, but definitely the best bite you've taken in a very long time.

5. Not making sliders? Serve this bacon on a salad. Even on ice cream. Tell your love handles they're welcome. Eat immediately or store on a wire rack in the fridge for up to 2 days to keep the texture nice and firm. You can keep at room temp for a half a day or so, but the warmer your kitchen is, the quicker the bacon will lose its texture.

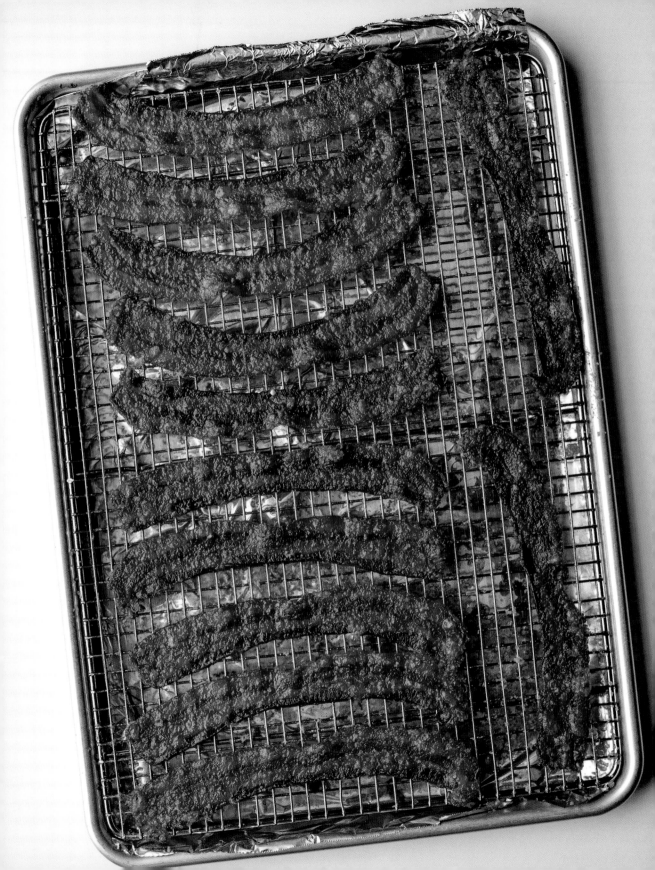

BLT Sliders with Candied Bacon

MAKES 12 SLIDERS

BLTs have succeeded for millennia because they are the epitome of true sandwich balance. Crispy, fatty bacon meets cool iceberg, creamy mayo, bright tomato, and soft, sweet bread. The addition of caramelized onions brings some much-needed funk to this sandwich, and since we're using candied bacon, it helps recalibrate the balance.

TIPS FROM THE SANDWICH KING: *Make sure that the bacon in your BLT is always crispy, whether using the candied variety or not. Limp bacon is a guaranteed Grade A sandwich destroyer.*

2 tablespoons vegetable oil

2 Maui (sweet) onions, cut into ¼-inch slices

Kosher salt

Freshly ground black pepper

8 tablespoons (1 stick) salted butter, at room
    temperature, for griddling

12 slider rolls (I like King's Hawaiian sweet rolls
    or Martin's potato rolls)

1 recipe Candied Bacon (page 32)

3 Roma tomatoes, cut into ¼-inch slices

4 crispy romaine lettuce leaves, each torn into
    3 pieces

1 recipe BBQ Rub Aioli (recipe follows)

1. Heat the oil in a large skillet over medium-low heat. Add the onions and gently sweat them out, stirring only occasionally, letting the sugars develop. If too much fond or crispy bits form on the bottom of the pan and are at risk of burning, deglaze with a couple splashes of water and scrape with a wooden spoon to help unstick the fond and incorporate it back into the onions. This develops a ton of flavor along the way. Cook until a deep golden brown, about 30 minutes. Season with salt and pepper and set aside.

2. As always, butter and griddle your bread! Set a large nonstick skillet over medium heat. Schmear butter on both insides of each bun and, working in batches, place butter side down on the skillet. Gently griddle until golden brown, about 5 minutes.

3. To build a sandwich, place a layer of the caramelized onions on the bottom half of a bun, followed by 2 halved pieces of pig candy, then tomato slices (seasoned with a bit of salt), 1 lettuce leaf, and a nice schmear of the aioli on the top bun *only*. Close and serve!

BBQ Rub Aioli

MAKES 1 CUP

1 cup mayonnaise
2 tablespoons The Best All-Purpose BBQ Rub
   (recipe follows)
1 tablespoon Dijon mustard

In a medium bowl, whisk the mayo, BBQ rub, and mustard until smooth. Refrigerate until used, for up to 2 weeks.

The Best All-Purpose BBQ Rub

MAKES ABOUT 2½ CUPS

1 cup turbinado sugar
½ cup granulated sugar
½ cup kosher salt
3 tablespoons chili powder
3 tablespoons smoked paprika
2 tablespoons granulated garlic
1 tablespoon onion powder
1½ teaspoons cayenne pepper
1 teaspoon ground cumin
1 teaspoon freshly ground black pepper

Mix all the ingredients together in a small bowl. Store in an airtight container in the pantry for up to 3 months.

This shot reminds me of the mezzanine seating at an opulent theater.

I refused to hire a hand model. I'm a "do your own stunts" kind of cookbook author.

The Most Addictive Sweet and Salty Nut Snack

MAKES ABOUT 2 CUPS

For some strange reason (constant hunger), I must always have a bowl of homemade roasted nuts at every get-together. Whether salty, sweet, herbaceous, or spicy, a jazzed-up bowl of fragrant roasted nuts always excites your guests. They're the perfect whistle-wetter to pair with a hoppy beer or big glass of chewy red wine, and they're wonderful on a charcuterie board as well, paired with cheese, fresh fruit, and pickled peppers.

SOMEWHAT SERIOUS TIP FROM A NOT-SO-SERIOUS GUY: *If you want to save some coin, bump up the spice level by upping the cayenne to ½ teaspoon. It will slow people down so the nuts last longer, and you'll have leftovers for the next day, when you can truly enjoy them.*

2 tablespoons unsalted butter
2 tablespoons unpacked light brown sugar
½ teaspoon kosher salt
½ cup whole raw almonds

½ cup whole raw cashews
½ cup unsalted peanuts
½ cup whole raw pecans
¼ teaspoon chili powder
¼ teaspoon ground cinnamon
¼ teaspoon ground cumin
⅛ teaspoon cayenne pepper
1 tablespoon roughly chopped fresh rosemary

1. Line a rimmed sheet pan with parchment paper.

2. Melt the butter and brown sugar in a large skillet over medium heat and add the salt. Add the almonds, cashews, peanuts, pecans, chili powder, cinnamon, cumin, and cayenne. Cook, stirring often, until the sugar is melted and the nuts are fragrant, 5 to 6 minutes. Add the rosemary and toss. Immediately spread the nut mixture on the prepared sheet pan.

3. Cool completely and serve, or store in an airtight container for up to 2 weeks in the pantry until your next guests pop in!

Pancetta and Parm Popcorn

MAKES ABOUT 8 CUPS

Popcorn and Chicago are best friends forever. In fact, not only was the popcorn machine invented here in Chicago, but so was the Chicago mix (Cheddar and caramel; see page 254) as well as Cracker Jacks. Popcorn is embedded deeply in our city's DNA, and if you don't believe that, I invite you to come watch me watch a movie at an actual movie theater, with a tub of popcorn between my legs.

It's a massacre. Popcorn everywhere . . . on my lap, on my sweater, in my mouth. Nothing is better than a couple of leftover "shirt corns" that you discover stuck to your shirt once you *think* the tub has run dry. It's like the surprise dessert course after the main dessert course in a high-end prix fixe tasting menu. It's why I go to the movie theater. Popcorn and previews.

AMAZING TIPS FROM AN AMAZING GUY:
This is a great appetizer for a party: salty, funky, and cheesy with just a bit of sweetness. It pairs amazingly with ice-cold Belgian ale while you're bingeing true-crime content.

1 pound thick-sliced (¼-inch) pancetta, diced
¾ cup good-quality popcorn kernels
1 tablespoon kosher salt
1 tablespoon packed light brown sugar
2 tablespoons unsalted butter, melted
1 cup shredded Parmigiano-Reggiano
    (about 4 ounces)

1. Place the pancetta in a cold large heavy-bottomed soup pot. Bring to medium heat and slowly render the pancetta, stirring occasionally until very crispy. Be careful not to burn. Set aside to drain on a paper towel–lined plate and reserve the fat in the pot.

2. Add three test kernels to the pot and cover. Once they pop, add the rest of the kernels and partially cover to let out steam. Once kernels start popping aggressively, shake the pot fairly vigorously back and forth to keep things moving. Make sure to not keep the cover completely sealed; always let it vent to ensure the popcorn stays light and crunchy and not saturated with moisture. When the popping frequency slows down, take the pot off the heat.

3. In a small food processor, blend the salt and sugar to create popcorn dust. Store extra dust in an airtight container in the pantry for your next popcorn session.

4. Drizzle the butter over the popcorn and stir, then add the pancetta, cheese, and a couple of pinches of the popcorn dust to taste. Shake vigorously to mix.

"Bone, Bone, Bone
Bone Bone Bone
Bone-less . . ." Bone
Thugs-n-Harmony

Pretzel-Coated Boneless Wings with Easy Cheese Sauce and Liquid Gold Honey-Mustard Sauce

MAKES 4 SERVINGS

When presented with the choice of regular bone-in wings or boneless wings, I usually opt for the boneless variety: first, better meat to crisp to sauce ratios and, second, zero waste. I do enjoy bone-in wings, but, man, often houseguests can get careless with their refuse, leaving bones strewn about the living room and glued to tiny paper plates with schmears of ranch and stray stalks of celery. This Buffalo boneyard can single-handedly decimate the smooth vibe of your well-prepared get-together.

This recipe combines all the fun flavors of a ball game: pretzel, cheese sauce, *and* mustard. These are a *slam dunk* every time.

NOTE: *The photo shows them deep fried, which is the recommended method. Baking is great, too! Just a little less naughty . . .*

1½ pounds chicken tenders or skinless, boneless breast halves, cut into 1½- to 2-inch pieces
½ cup Liquid Gold Honey-Mustard Sauce (page 116), plus more for serving
Nonstick cooking spray, or 2 cups vegetable oil if you're frying the tenders
1 cup all-purpose flour
3 large eggs, whisked
1½ cups finely pulverized salted pretzels (about the consistency of coarse Lake Michigan sand, not white powder tropical beach sand)
Easiest Cheese Sauce of All Time (page 42), for serving

1. Place the chicken in a gallon zip-top bag with the honey-mustard sauce and squish the sauce all around to incorporate. Marinate in the refrigerator for at least 2 hours and up to 8 hours.
2. Adjust an oven rack to the middle position and preheat the oven to 450°F. Spray a rimmed sheet pan with nonstick cooking spray and set a wire rack in the pan. Alternatively, preheat the vegetable oil in a deep fryer to 350°F.
3. Create a breading line with three separate large shallow bowls. Place the flour in the first bowl, the whisked eggs in the second, and the pretzels in the third. Working with one tender at a time, use one hand to dredge it in the flour, shaking off any excess. Use your other hand to dip the tender in the eggs, coating it completely. Use your dry hand to evenly coat the tender with the pulverized pretzels.
4. If baking, place the coated chicken on the prepared sheet pan. Bake for 12 to 14 minutes, or until the internal temp registers 165°F. If frying, place the chicken gently in the oil and fry in batches for 4 to 5 minutes a side, or until golden and the internal temperature reaches 165°F.
5. Serve with more honey-mustard sauce and a sidecar of cheese sauce.

Easiest Cheese Sauce of All Time

This cheese sauce is as close as you're going to get to canned orange (or maybe yellowish) nacho cheese sauce. I have a special place in my heart for canned, weirdly neon orange/yellow cheese sauce. I remember in grade school we would often luncheon at the Italian beef stand down the street. Called Annie's Beef, it was run by the friendliest Korean guy named Simon and his wife, and while their Italian beef sandwiches were somewhat dismal, their burgers were on point—char-grilled to order and totally delicious. Especially with a side of cheese fries.

These were the pale yet crispy fry variety served in a flimsy paper boat with a 3-ounce Styrofoam cup of bright orange cheese sauce. Because we were young, mischievous boys, we would often have cheese fry races, which involved flinging cheese-covered fries at the wall to see which one would slide and fall down first. Come to think of it, that was a pretty dicky move and totally unacceptable. I'm so very sorry, Simon . . . You deserved better than that.

This cheese sauce is by far the most *stable* cheese sauce I've ever made. It doesn't break, clump, or get grainy. It's great on nachos and grilled cheeseburgers, as a base for stovetop mac and cheese, and for adhering fries to the wall of your local fast-food joint (just be sure to clean up after yourself).

TOP-NOTCH TIPS FROM YOUR PAL JEFF:
You can experiment with different kinds of cheese, but always do two things: Grate your own (the pregrated stuff just doesn't melt the same due to its anticaking agents), and always choose one creamier melting cheese (Fontina, Jack,

American, Velveeta) and one salty and sharp cheese (Cheddar, Asiago, blue, Gouda). And no stringy melting cheese like mozzarella!

One 12-ounce can evaporated milk
2 teaspoons Dijon mustard
1 teaspoon hot sauce, such as Cholula
1 cup freshly grated sharp Cheddar (about 4 ounces)
½ cup freshly grated pepper Jack (about 2 ounces)
2 ounces blue cheese, freshly crumbled
1 tablespoon cornstarch whisked with 2 tablespoons water, as needed for thickening

1. Set a medium saucepan over low heat. Add the evaporated milk, mustard, and hot sauce and whisk until smooth. Bring to a light simmer and then slowly whisk in the cheeses. Lightly simmer until the sauce thickens, stirring constantly for about 5 minutes, until all the cheese is melted and the sauce is silky and smooth. If you need to thicken the sauce, whisk in a little cornstarch slurry and simmer until the desired thickness is achieved.

2. This cheese sauce can hold on the stove over very low heat until ready to serve. If you need to make it in advance, just cool to room temperature and store in an airtight container in the fridge. When it's time to reheat, place in a small saucepan over medium heat, add 2 to 3 tablespoons milk, and whisk vigorously until you smooth things out and the cheese sauce is fully warmed through, about 10 minutes.

Nacho "Boil"

As landlocked children in the Chicagoland area, we didn't experience shrimp boils, crab boils, lobster boils, or any saltwater seafood-based boils, for that matter. Therefore, we missed out on this dump-on-the-table-style communal way of eating. But I'm going to be honest—I'd rather chow down on cheesy chorizo nachos than boiled shrimp any day of the week. And that is why this recipe exists. It's as fun to plate and serve as it is to eat.

Go crazy with this. Do it free form like Jackson Pollock or get cubist like Picasso. Just remember, no gussied-up chip will taste the same; each will be a different eating experience. That's the beauty of nachos.

NOT SO MUCH A TIP FROM JEFF BUT RATHER A BRILLIANT OBSERVATION:
Nachos are the snowflake of food. No two are alike.

Two 14-ounce tubes chorizo, casings removed
One 15-ounce can black beans, drained and
    rinsed
1 teaspoon ground cumin
1 teaspoon chili powder
Two 16-ounce bags good-quality, super-hearty
    tortilla chips
1 recipe Easiest Cheese Sauce of All Time
    (page 42)
1 cup sour cream

4 green onions, thinly sliced on the bias
2 Roma tomatoes, cut into a small dice
1 cup chopped fresh cilantro
1 cup drained pickled sliced jalapeños

1. Place the chorizo in a medium nonstick pan over medium-high heat. Cook for 10 minutes, stirring a couple of times to break up the meat, until the chorizo is cooked through and slightly browned. Use a slotted spoon to scoop the chorizo onto paper towels to absorb the fat, reserving 1 tablespoon of the fat in the pan.
2. Add the beans, cumin, and chili powder to the pan and cook until heated through, about 5 minutes, stirring occasionally.
3. Cover your table with long sheets of parchment or peach paper.«
4. Plan on two layers of nachos! Spread an even layer of chips over the parchment. Sprinkle half the chorizo and beans over the chips, then ladle half the warm cheese sauce over the top. Repeat with another layer of chips, chorizo, beans, and cheese sauce. Top with a bunch of tablespoon-size dollops of sour cream, the green onions, tomatoes, cilantro, and jalapeños.
5. Make all your loved ones wash the bejesus out of their hands, and then sound a blowhorn to signify the start of this event. *Do not let anyone leave until it's all gone.*

« This is the size of a medium folding table.

Sweet and Sticky and Crispy Korean Chicken Wings

MAKES 4 SERVINGS

The magic of these delectable wings is that once they are coated in the sauce and butter, they stay crispy and saturated with flavor for a good 10 minutes, just enough time for you and yours to devour them with minimal breaks for breathing. The double-fry method makes these not only super crispy but also easier to make ahead.

WING TIPS: *Have a bone bowl nearby to prevent the inevitable cleaned-wing boneyard around the app table. Keep all that unsightly rubbish centralized and easily dumpable.*

Canola oil, for frying
2 garlic cloves
One 1-inch piece ginger, peeled
3 tablespoons soy sauce
3 tablespoons gochujang (Korean chile paste)
1½ tablespoons rice vinegar
1 tablespoon Asian untoasted sesame oil
1 tablespoon honey
2 tablespoons unsalted butter
16 chicken wings (about 1¾ pounds), flats and
    drums separated
Kosher salt and freshly ground black pepper
½ cup all-purpose flour
½ cup cornstarch
1 teaspoon baking powder
¼ cup sesame seeds, toasted
2 green onions, thinly sliced on the bias

1. Heat 2 inches of canola oil to 350°F in a 6-quart heavy-bottomed pot over medium-high heat.

2. Using a Microplane, grate the garlic and ginger into a medium saucepan over medium heat. Add the soy sauce, gochujang, vinegar, sesame oil, and honey and bring to a simmer for 5 minutes, until thickened slightly. Mix in the butter and transfer the sauce to a large metal bowl.

3. Season the chicken with salt and pepper. Whisk the flour, cornstarch, baking powder, and 1 cup water in a large bowl. Add the chicken and toss until coated, then toss the chicken in a strainer to remove all but a thin layer of the cornstarch mixture.

4. Working in batches, fry the chicken until golden, 6 to 8 minutes. Drain on paper towels and rest for 1 hour or up to 3 days in the fridge, covered. Return the oil to 350°F. Fry the chicken again until crisp, 6 to 8 minutes more. Drain again.

5. Toss the chicken in the sauce and garnish with toasted sesame seeds and green onions. Serve immediately and eat immediately. Wings are best served hot and crispy.

Again, I didn't bring in a stunt eater to work on these wings. This was all me.

Sub "Boil"

Much like the Nacho "Boil" (page 45), this is what most health experts would categorize as an "abomination." Who cares what the fitness bloggers may or may not think of this ridiculously fun-to-make and even more fun-to-eat free-form party sub? So slap on your nacho bib, squeeze into some yoga pants, and eat like the legendary athlete you were born to be.

DA TIPS: *Cleanup is as easy as just rolling up the paper and tossing it right in the garbage.*

½ pound pancetta, cut into ½-inch cubes

6 soft Italian rolls or sub rolls, cut on the bias into "nacho chips"

Olive oil

1 head iceberg lettuce, very thinly sliced

1 cup freshly grated Asiago (about 4 ounces)

½ pound shaved mortadella with pistachios

½ pound gabagool chiffonade (thinly sliced capicola stacked and cut into chiffonade)

½ pound Genoa salami, cut into see-through slices

2 to 3 Roma tomatoes, cut into a small dice

1¼ cups Homemade Real Giardiniera (page 244) or one 10-ounce jar oil-packed store-bought, oil strained and reserved for another use

8 ounces mozzarella, cut into a small dice

One 10-ounce squeeze bottle sweet Italian vinaigrette

1. Adjust an oven rack to the middle position and preheat the oven to broil.

2. Set a medium skillet over medium heat and add the pancetta. When the pancetta starts to sizzle, stir every minute or so, until golden brown, about 10 minutes. Drain on a paper towel–lined plate.

3. Generously douse the rolls with oil in a large bowl. Spread them out on a sheet pan and broil until just golden brown, with some give and chew left in.

4. Cover a table with a ton of parchment or peach paper.

5. Layer a long mound of the iceberg evenly over the covered table. Spread the golden-brown sub "chips" over the lettuce. Then on goes the cheese, then the meats, *ribboned* around, creating more height. Make a layer of the tomatoes and giardiniera. Add a nice sprinkle of the bocconcini over the spread. Finally, with the squeeze bottle, douse it in vinaigrette.

6. Ring the bell and beckon the kids. Serve with BBQ chips and a 12-pack of Peroni. Don't forget your sub bib, either.

« This is exactly how I first pictured this "dish" in a sweaty fever dream.

Hoodie courtesy of BSTV, the producers of *The Kitchen*. Apron courtesy of my friends in Lagos, Nigeria.

3

Come On Over!

I'M THROWING AN ISLAND PARTY

This chapter is not necessarily a replacement for a much-needed tropical vacation to the islands, but by golly, it's fun food that might evoke memories of more relaxed sun-and-rum-filled times.

Jerk Pan Jerk Chicken for a Crowd

MAKES 6 TO 8 SERVINGS

This recipe was provided by my favorite Caymanians, Luigi and Christina Moaxam, who are not only friends but also the owners of my favorite restaurant in Grand Cayman: Cayman Cabana. We've been traveling to Cayman for the last decade with my aunt Jae and uncle Dave and our cousins Dave, Joe, Danny, and Jenny, who may have never really officially invited us on the trips.

As a consolation for our glomming on to their vacations, I treated the family to a jerk chicken extravaganza, made by Luigi and his chefs, right at our condo on Seven Mile Beach. They rolled in their jerk pan (what they call their smoky charcoal grill), fired it up, and started slow-grilling these beautiful pieces of super-marinated chicken.

We drank cold Caybrews while watching the sun set over the aquamarine Caribbean. The smell of jerk smoke and charred chicken skin intoxicated us even further. The chicken was the best I've ever had. Luigi and Christina have been kind enough to share with me their recipe, which is always best when marinated overnight in the fridge.

½ cup firmly packed dark brown sugar

½ cup ground allspice

10 seasoning peppers or mini multicolored bell peppers (they should be mild; see Note)

6 Scotch bonnet peppers

8 garlic cloves

2 bunches of green onions

2 tablespoons fresh thyme leaves

1 tablespoon whole allspice berries

1 teaspoon ground cinnamon

½ teaspoon ground nutmeg

¼ cup orange or pineapple juice (fresh is great, but bottled is fine)

2 tablespoons olive oil

Kosher salt

1 teaspoon freshly ground black pepper

2 tablespoons soy sauce, as needed

One 5- to 6-pound chicken, cut into quarters (leg/thigh and breast/wing)

Vegetable oil, for greasing

Sliced white bread and ketchup, for serving

1. Place the brown sugar, allspice, peppers, garlic, green onions, thyme, allspice berries, cinnamon, nutmeg, juice, olive oil, 1 tablespoon salt, and black pepper in a food processor. Blend until a thick paste is formed, clingy enough to stick to the back of spoon. If it's too thick, thin with the soy sauce.

2. Scrape the paste into a large zip-top bag and add the chicken. Zip the bag and squish the paste all around, making sure each piece of chicken gets a little attention. Marinate in the fridge overnight, up to 24 hours.

3. Prepare the grill with one hot and one unheated side. This works best with a charcoal grill or at the very least a gas grill with a smoker box (see page 98 for a smoker box tutorial).

4. Remove the chicken from the marinade to a large bowl and season with a bit of salt. Oil the grill grates liberally with the vegetable oil, and place the chicken skin side up on the cool side of the grill and close the lid. Grill for 30 to 35 minutes, or until the breasts register 160°F and the thighs register 165°F. Be sure to rotate the pieces every 10 minutes to ensure even exposure to the hot side of the grill.

5. Move the chicken to the hot side of the grill, flip it skin side down, and grill for 6 to 8 minutes, until the skin is charred and crispy and the chicken hits an internal temp of 165°F for the breast and 170°F for the thighs.

6. Serve immediately with some good ol' white bread from the bag and ketchup to dunk it in and stare off into the sea while the warm Caribbean breeze gently tickles your beach-purchased vacation cornrows.

NOTE: *The original recipe calls for "seasoning peppers," which I haven't been able to find here in the States.*

Stare at this shot for sixty seconds and your nose will start to tingle.

Coconut Rice

MAKES 4 TO 6 SERVINGS

Here is my confession. I suck at making rice. Maybe it's because I didn't grow up eating rice. Maybe it's because I called in sick that day in culinary school. Maybe it's because I'm a heavy-handed, sausage-fingered buffoon who wouldn't know finesse if she asked me to slow dance at my eighth-grade coed mixer during an encore spinning of "More Than Words" (my jam).

Regardless, this is the only rice recipe I have successfully made in my home kitchen. Food scientists may conclude it's because of that wonderful coconut fat and how the lipids coat each grain of rice with a protective yet delectable layer, ensuring fluffier and more evenly cooked grains of rice. That may be true, but I also think the subtle tropical aroma and addictive texture of the crunchy shredded coconut instantly transport me via Economy Plus far, far away to the warmth and peace of Seven Mile Beach.

2 cups jasmine rice, rinsed under cold water
    until water runs clear
1½ tablespoons coconut oil
One 13.5-ounce can full-fat coconut milk, well
    shaken
2 teaspoons kosher salt
1 teaspoon sugar
1 cup shredded unsweetened coconut
Fresh lime slices, for serving
1 teaspoon lime zest, for serving

1. Preheat the oven to 350°F.
2. Add the rice to a medium saucepan (one you have a matching lid for!). Spoon in the coconut oil and mix it into the rice. This creates a nice fat barrier to ensure well-separated grains of rice.
3. Add the coconut milk, salt, and 2 cups water to the pot. Give it a good stir and cover with a lid. Bring to a boil, then immediately reduce the heat to a gentle simmer. Simmer for 10 minutes, remove from the heat with the lid still on, and let the rice rest for 15 minutes.
4. While the rice is cooking, place the shredded coconut on a parchment-lined sheet pan. Bake for 8 to 10 minutes, until golden brown and crispy. Let cool.
5. Fluff the rice with a fork and serve garnished with fresh lime slices, the lime zest, and a nice topping of toasted coconut.

Serve in a coconut for
extra credit!

Luigi's Coconut Ceviche

MAKES 4 SERVINGS

When Luigi served this to me at his famed farm-to-table dinner at Cayman Cabana, I could have sworn I was eating scallop or squid ceviche pulled straight from the Caribbean. The flavors and textures are so pure and bright. It's truly addictive and worth the search for a whole young coconut. I am honoring the island way and the original recipe, but chances are, you will not find seasoning peppers in most cities. Opt for a bag of mini multicolored sweet bell peppers instead!

But before attempting to open the coconut, do as any intelligent adult would do and search YouTube for a quality tutorial.

2 whole young coconuts, meat scooped from the inside using a spoon and cut into long strips (see Note on Coconut)

3 seasoning peppers or mini multicolored bell peppers (they should be mild), cored, seeded, and cut into a small dice

1 Scotch bonnet pepper, finely diced (wear gloves when dicing, please!)

1 green onion, thinly sliced on the bias

¼ cup chiffonade fresh culantro (see Note on Culantro), cilantro, or mint

¼ cup fresh lime juice (from about 2 limes)

½ teaspoon kosher salt

¼ teaspoon freshly ground black pepper

1 teaspoon olive oil

Crispy Plantain Chips (page 58), for serving

1. Combine the coconut, peppers, onion, culantro, lime juice, salt, pepper, and oil in a medium bowl and marinate for at least 30 minutes.

2. Taste and adjust seasoning with salt and pepper, if necessary, and serve with chips alongside.

NOTE ON COCONUT: *Fresh young coconut meat is best from a whole white coconut that comes plastic-wrapped and ready to open. This is not the fuzzy brown variety. Those are much harder to open (see Tom Hanks in* Castaway*)! Trader Joe's usually has them.*

NOTE ON CULANTRO: *My man Luigi calls for culantro in this recipe, which is grown in tropical regions and is very similar in flavor and aroma to cilantro. If you don't live on the islands, then cilantro is just perfect.*

Crispy Plantain Chips

MAKES 4 SERVINGS

The first time I had legit fried plantains was from a roadside "soda," or small store, in Costa Rica. We stopped to grab some coconut water right from the nut, some ridiculous chicharróns, and a bag of local fried plantains. Saw my first wild crocodile on that stop. Then saw my first wild toucan. Then a wild scarlet macaw. Then another toucan, then a flock of scarlet macaws!

Sarah, Lorenzo, and I sat on the roadside while munching on a bag of these slightly sweet and salty plantains and taking swigs of cold fresh coconut water. We stared up at all these magnificent wild creatures I'd traveled so far to see, one of them my all-time favorite bird—a scarlet macaw. What a scene!

Full disclosure: I am a reformed Bird Nerd. Growing up, I was a giant fan of birds, especially parrots. Not only did I own a silvery gray cockatiel named Pee-Wee, but I also was a loyal subscriber to *Bird Talk* magazine. I obsessed and fantasized about owning a tropical menagerie of all kinds of colorful parrots. Conures, African greys, yellow-fronted amazons—I would picture myself coming home from school and throwing my backpack on the ground while a flock of birds landed on my head, shoulders, and fingers.

I loved the intelligence and coloring of these far-from-midwestern species. Never in a million years would Pam or Gus let me keep a big-beaked, unbelievably loud, poop-shooting parrot in our family home. Therefore, a monthly subscription to *Bird Talk* and a cockatiel named Pee-Wee with a shoe fetish had to do.

When I discovered the mystery of the opposite sex and the majesty of rock and roll, I quickly changed my subscription from *Bird Talk* to *Rolling Stone*. I moved on from my bird phase but never stopped loving my own bird. Pee-Wee lived to see eighteen years of age before passing away quietly in the night. He is currently buried in a shoe box with his favorite gym shoe in the backyard of my parents' old house. He was a good bird.

I think I love plantains because I love birds so much, ya know?

Canola oil, for frying
3 green plantains
1 teaspoon black peppercorns
1 teaspoon kosher salt

1. Fill a large Dutch oven halfway with oil and heat it to 350°F over medium heat.
2. Peel the plantains and slice them lengthwise into long, thin strips (a mandoline will give you the best results).
3. Crack the peppercorns by crushing them with a heavy pan on a cutting board; you are looking for a very coarse grind.
4. Working in batches, gently lay the plantain strips into the hot oil and fry them until crispy, about 1 minute. Transfer the plantains directly to a paper towel–lined plate, immediately season with the salt and crushed pepper, and serve.

Mango and Avocado Salad

MAKES 4 TO 6 SERVINGS

Is this a dip or a salad? That is for the *chip* to decide. If a heaping tablespoon of dip on a single crunchy chip is too much for the chip to handle and it breaks, then it's a salad.

By all means, don't let that stop you from serving this as an appetizer with a big bowl of very strong tortilla chips.

2 tablespoons fresh lime juice
¼ cup olive oil
1 teaspoon kosher salt
2 tablespoons agave syrup
2 mangoes, peeled and cut into a ½-inch dice
¼ cup small-diced red onion
¼ cup roughly chopped fresh cilantro, plus a few leaves for garnish
1 bird's eye or Thai chile, sliced into thin rings
6 small or 3 medium ripe avocados
½ cup toasted salted pumpkin seeds

1. Combine the lime juice, oil, salt, and agave syrup in a medium bowl. Whisk vigorously until the dressing becomes thick. Set aside.

2. Build your beautiful salad in a large bowl. Combine the mangoes, onion, cilantro, and chile (this chile is hot, so add a little, then more to taste). I wait until everything else is ready to go before preparing the avocados, as nobody likes brown avocados. Peel and pit the avocados and cut them into a medium dice. Gently fold them in.

3. Drizzle in the dressing and, with a rubber spatula, gently fold everything together; those avocados are fragile, just like my heart.

4. Now, to finish off this piece of artwork, transfer the salad to a colorful serving bowl and sprinkle on the pumpkin seeds and a few leaves of cilantro. It's the perfect dip . . . er . . . salad . . . I mean dish . . . for any island party!

Grilled Blackened Snapper Escovitch with Mango Aioli

MAKES 4 SERVINGS

Escovitch is a Jamaican term which usually refers to frying the fish and serving it with pickled peppers, onions, pimentón, and all the accompanying pickling liquid. It's a heck of a combo, and once you taste it, you'll literally start using up all your miles to fly back to the islands so you can eat it again.

In this version, we are blackening and pan-frying with good ol' butter—no deep frying needed. One bite of the smoky, buttery fish with the colorful mélange of peppers and you'll be instantly teleported to your favorite island resort. In fact, the main side effect of this dish is a vivid dream of quietly rolling out of bed at your favorite 3.5-star all-inclusive resort at 6:00 AM so as to not wake your loved ones and then grabbing some towels, flip-flops, and magazines in order to save some chairs by that prime area at the pool.

3 tablespoons Blackening Spices for Any- and Everything (recipe follows on page 64)
3 tablespoons unsalted butter
Four 4- to 6-ounce snapper fillets, pin bones and skins removed

1 tablespoon vegetable oil
1 recipe Pickled Escovitch Peppers (recipe follows on page 64)
1 recipe Mango Aioli (recipe follows on page 64)

1. Combine the blackening spices and butter in a small microwave-safe bowl. Cover with a wet paper towel and microwave on high for 45 seconds. Take out, whisk, and set aside to cool completely.

2. Coat both sides of the fish with the blackening spices and butter mixture.

3. Heat the oil in a large nonstick skillet over medium-high heat. Add the fish and cook 5 minutes on each side, until both sides are charred and the internal temp hits 135°F. Don't disturb the fish while it's cooking!

4. Divide the escovitch peppers among serving plates and top with the fish. Serve with the aioli on the side so diners can dollop it on the fish.

Pickled Escovitch Peppers

MAKES ONE 16-OUNCE JAR

1½ cups apple cider vinegar
⅓ cup sugar
1 tablespoon honey
1 fresh tarragon sprig
2 fresh thyme sprigs
1 teaspoon black peppercorns
2 tablespoons kosher salt
1 red bell pepper, cored, seeded, and cut into
   ¼-inch strips
1 orange bell pepper, cored, seeded, and cut
   into ¼-inch strips
1 yellow bell pepper, cored, seeded, and cut
   into ¼-inch strips
1 jalapeño, cored, seeded, and cut into ¼-inch
   strips
½ medium yellow onion, thinly sliced

1. Combine the vinegar, sugar, honey, tarragon, thyme, peppercorns, and salt in a medium saucepan. Simmer for 5 minutes to intensify the flavors and dissolve the sugar.
2. Turn off the heat and add the peppers and onion.
3. Let cool to room temperature, about 15 minutes. You most definitely serve these warm with the fish. Keep leftover peppers in the fridge in an airtight container for up to 1 week.

Mango Aioli

MAKES 1¼ CUPS

1 cup mayonnaise
¼ cup mango chutney
Zest and juice of 1 lime
Kosher salt and freshly ground black pepper

Combine the mayo, chutney, and lime zest and juice in a small bowl and season with salt and pepper to taste. This will keep in an airtight container in the fridge for up to a week. It's also really good on turkey and bacon club sandwiches or to dunk chicken nuggets into.

Blackening Spices for Any- and Everything

MAKES ABOUT 1 CUP

2 tablespoons kosher salt
1 to 2 teaspoons cayenne pepper
2 tablespoons chili powder
2 tablespoons smoked paprika
2 tablespoons freshly ground black pepper
2 tablespoons onion powder
2 tablespoons granulated garlic
2 tablespoons dried thyme
2 tablespoons dried oregano

1. Place all the ingredients into a spice grinder or food processer and pulse until fine and uniform.
2. Store in an airtight container in the pantry for up to 3 months.

Takeout-Style Chinese Spare Ribs

MAKES 4 SERVINGS

Chinese-American takeout spare ribs always look better than they taste. They're super red, super shiny, and super sticky, but the meat is always just too tough and the flavor one note. This version has that "don't look directly at the rib or you'll burn your retina" bright red color but with complex layers of flavor and a tender and supple texture.

Although this recipe calls for grilling, these spare ribs can also be made in the oven. Just place on a well-greased wire-racked parchment-lined sheet pan and cook at 250°F for 3 hours, or until tender and caramelized.

They are best when marinated overnight in the fridge, so plan accordingly.

¼ cup soy sauce

½ cup hoisin sauce

3 tablespoons Chinese rice wine

2 tablespoons dark brown sugar

1 tablespoon five-spice powder

1 teaspoon granulated garlic

1 teaspoon freshly grated peeled ginger

¾ teaspoon red food coloring

4 to 5 tablespoons honey

2 racks spare ribs (St. Louis–style works best), about 6 pounds total, sliced into single ribs

1. Whisk together the soy sauce, hoisin, rice wine, brown sugar, five-spice powder, garlic, ginger, food coloring, and 2 tablespoons of the honey in a medium bowl. Pour the marinade into a large zip-top bag, reserving ½ cup for basting later. Place the ribs in the bag, seal it, and marinate overnight if possible but at least for 3 hours.

2. Remove the ribs from the marinade bag (discard the marinade) and place them on a sheet pan fitted with a wire rack. The sheet pan keeps any drippings off your counter and the wire rack makes it easy to transfer and cook neatly on the grill.

3. Preheat grill to 275°F and place the wire rack directly on the grill. Cook for 2 to 3 hours, until very tender, basting frequently with the reserved marinade to develop that candy-red shellac.

4. Drizzle the ribs with the remaining 2 to 3 tablespoons honey (to taste) and rotate each rib meaty side down. Place the rack on the hot side of the grill to give it one final round of caramelization, 3 to 5 minutes.

Now those are red ribs!

Hawaiian BBQ Pork Extravaganza

MAKES 8 TO 10 SERVINGS

When I had just turned sixteen, Gus and Pam took us kids on our first tropical vacation. They cashed in a bunch of coupons and got a really great deal at a beautiful resort in Maui. My cousins, the Bernis, went too, and I'd never been more excited.

I was sporting a brand-new Discman and an updated physique thanks to a two-week crash diet called Cybergenics, where all I did was do high-impact group aerobics and eat cold chicken breasts.

My brother, Frank, and I and our two cousins Joe and Dave all shared our own suite. We quickly discovered the power of charging things to the room, mainly bottles of mai tai mix from the gift store and outrageously priced rum-packed pineapple cocktails served in actual pineapples with at least six straws.

We were a long way from our usual vacation at a friend's cottage on a lake in Wisconsin or at the Holidome in Rockford, Illinois, and the excitement was nonstop. We swam, snorkeled, and surfed. We sunned and snacked, and some of us burned. I tasted my first Kalua pork at a thrilling beachfront luau. I'll never forget the aroma of that succulent swine as it was pulled, right there in front of us, from the banana leaf–lined charcoal pit it was roasted in. I'll also never forget the first bite of that slightly sweet and buttery-soft pork. Nor will I ever forget the look of the server who handled the pork station as I went up for my fourth and final helping.

¼ cup packed light brown sugar

2 tablespoons kosher salt

1 tablespoon freshly ground black pepper

1 tablespoon Chinese five-spice powder

1 teaspoon garlic powder

1 tablespoon ground ginger

1 tablespoon onion powder

One 5-pound boneless pork shoulder or butt, fat cap scored deep in a crosshatch pattern

8 tablespoons (1 stick) salted butter, at room temperature, for griddling

One 8-count package sweet rolls (I like King's Hawaiian sweet rolls)

SWEET CHILE SAUCE

½ cup rice vinegar

¼ cup packed light brown sugar

¼ teaspoon kosher salt

1 to 2 tablespoons red pepper flakes, or to taste

1 tablespoon freshly grated peeled ginger

1 garlic clove, grated

FOR SERVING

2 or 3 tablespoons salted butter, at room temperature

1 recipe Pickled Cukes and Carrots (recipe follows)

1 recipe Sweet and Hot Honey Hot Mustard (recipe follows)

1. Mix the brown sugar, salt, pepper, five-spice powder, garlic powder, ginger, and onion powder in a medium bowl. Rub the spice mix over the entire pork. Place the pork on a sheet pan fitted with a wire rack, cover with plastic wrap, and refrigerate for at least 2 hours. If you have the time, let it sit in the fridge overnight—it will make a world of difference.

2. Adjust an oven rack to the middle position and preheat the oven to 325°F. Remove the plastic wrap and cover the pork with a layer of parchment paper, then a layer of aluminum foil and roast for 3 hours.

3. Remove the pork from the oven, uncover, and drain any liquid fat from the pan. Return to the oven, uncovered, and roast until the internal temperature reaches 200°F and the pork is well browned, about 1½ hours more.

4. When the pork is almost ready, make the sweet chile sauce. In a medium saucepan over medium heat, bring the vinegar, brown sugar, and salt to a boil, then simmer until thickened and reduced by half, about 15 minutes. Remove from the heat and stir in the red pepper flakes, ginger, and garlic.

5. Transfer the pork to a large dish, pour the sweet chile sauce on top, cover with foil, and let rest for 20 minutes. Using two forks, pull apart the pork.

6. As always, butter and griddle your bread! Set a large nonstick skillet over medium heat. Schmear butter on both insides of each bun and, working in batches, place butter side down on the skillet. Gently griddle until golden brown, about 5 minutes.

7. Serve the pork in a build-your-own style with a plate of rolls and bowls of the pickles and honey mustard.

Pickled Cukes and Carrots

MAKES 4 CUPS

2 cups rice vinegar
¼ cup sugar
2 teaspoons kosher salt
1 cup shredded carrots (from about 2 medium carrots, but I buy the preshredded carrots—so much easier!)
1 cup ¼-inch half-moon-sliced English cucumbers
1 teaspoon red pepper flakes

1. Bring 1 cup water, the vinegar, sugar, and salt to a boil in a medium saucepan over medium-high heat. Stir well to ensure the sugar has dissolved. Remove from the heat and add the carrots, cucumbers, and red pepper flakes. Let sit for at least 30 minutes. This is referred to as "quick pickling" or "ain't got the time to pickle!"

2. Store in an airtight container in the fridge for up to 1 month.

Sweet and Hot Honey Hot Mustard

MAKES 1 CUP

¼ cup ground mustard powder
¼ cup boiling water
2 tablespoons honey
1 tablespoon toasted sesame oil
1 tablespoon vegetable oil
½ teaspoon kosher salt

1. Very easy! Mix all the ingredients in a small bowl until mustardy, smooth, and lump-free.

2. Store in an airtight container in the fridge for up to 2 weeks.

Sweet Potato Potato Salad

MAKES 6 TO 8 SERVINGS

I had this for the first time in Cayman at a little roadside chicken joint appropriately named "Chicken! Chicken!" and I was hooked. I've had gallons of potato salad over the years, but never did I have a potato salad made with sweet potatoes! I took a bite and had an epiphany. It's brighter, sunnier, and more festive than the standard potato salad and it deserves a spot at all your summer BBQs from here on out.

2 celery stalks, cut into small dice

½ small red onion, minced

½ cup mayonnaise

¼ cup roughly chopped gherkins

Zest and juice of 1 lemon

2 tablespoons whole-grain mustard

1 tablespoon honey

Kosher salt and freshly ground black pepper

2 pounds sweet potatoes, peeled and cut into 1-inch chunks

¼ cup white vinegar

2 tablespoons minced fresh chives

2 tablespoons minced fresh flat-leaf parsley

1. Mix together the celery, onion, mayo, gherkins, lemon zest and juice, mustard, and honey in a large bowl. Season with ¾ tablespoon salt and ½ teaspoon pepper and let sit while the potatoes cook. This mellows out the onion while marrying all the rest of the flavors with the mayo.

2. Place the potatoes in a large saucepan and add enough cold water to cover by 1 inch. Season the water generously with salt. Bring to a boil over medium-high heat. Once at a boil, reduce the heat to a simmer and cook until the potatoes are tender, about 10 minutes.

3. Drain the potatoes in a colander and, while still piping hot, add the vinegar. (It's okay if some falls through the colander; plenty will penetrate the potatoes.) The hot potatoes will soak in all that vinegar flavor, seasoning each potato top to bottom. Using a rubber spatula, toss gently to combine.

4. Add the warm potatoes to the bowl with the dressing and toss with the chives and parsley. Season to taste with more salt and pepper. Serve immediately or store in an airtight container overnight. I prefer freshly mixed, slightly warm potato salad, so my vote is to serve it fresh. However, some people prefer the flavor when it has had a chance to chill out overnight in the fridge. If you do serve it the next day, be sure to adjust the seasoning, if necessary, with more salt and pepper.

How often do you look at a potato salad and proclaim out loud, "That's a beautiful potato salad!"?

4

I'M HOSTING LORENZO'S BIRTHDAY . . . LORD HELP ME

Children's birthday parties are my least favorite kind of party. Gaggles of rambunctious sugar-pumped children make a mess and generally drain all the life force out of your body and soul until it's time to feed them each a final slice of insulin-spiking cake, throw them a Mylar bag full of crappy tchotchkes, and finally hand them off to their legal guardians, exhausted and nauseated. The thing is, all parents must eventually succumb to this, so when it's your time to host and celebrate your little one's birthday, you might as well do it *right* and make the best food possible, so at least when the fog has cleared and the last of the lingering parents have left, you can make yourself your own plate of deliciousness and bask in the glory of being the best cook on the block.

Baked Coconut Chicken Tenders

MAKES 4 SERVINGS

Kids love tenders. Adults love kids who order tenders. Kids hate fathers who want them to order tenders just so the father can steal two or three of the kid's tenders.

Here's a great way to provide a healthier tender for your kids that everyone at the table can enjoy, regardless of age.

½ cup coconut flour, almond flour, or
   all-purpose flour
2 large eggs
½ cup light coconut milk or 2% milk
1½ cups whole wheat panko crumbs
1 cup desiccated or shredded unsweetened
   coconut
1 teaspoon kosher salt
½ teaspoon freshly ground black pepper
2 pounds chicken tenders, patted dry
Olive oil cooking spray

DIPPING SAUCE
1 cup mango chutney
¼ cup sour cream or whole milk Greek yogurt

1. Preheat the oven to 400°F. Line a rimmed sheet pan with parchment paper and add a wire rack on top.
2. Create a breading line with three separate medium shallow bowls. Place the flour in the first bowl. In the second bowl, whisk the eggs and milk. In the third bowl, stir together the panko, coconut, salt, and pepper to combine. Working with one tender at a time, use one hand to dredge it in the flour, shaking off any excess. Use your other hand to dip the tender in the egg mixture, coating it completely. Use your dry hand to evenly coat the tender with the panko mixture. Place it on the prepared wire rack. Repeat to bread the rest of the tenders.
3. Spray the tenders with cooking spray. Bake for 18 to 20 minutes, until golden brown and cooked through (if the breading is light in color, turn on the broiler for the last 2 minutes of cooking time).
4. To make the dipping sauce, whisk the chutney and sour cream in a small bowl.
5. Serve the tenders with the dipping sauce!

United States of Meat Loaf

MAKES 4 TO 6 SERVINGS

This is the best meat loaf I've ever had. It's all in taking the extra step to sauté your onions and vegetables so they just melt into the loaf of meat. Plus, by adding saltine crackers instead of boring old white bread or bread crumbs, you're bumping up the flavor and texture. Those little crackers just soak up so much moisture and add a silky texture without being too bready or dense. This is one great meat loaf. So great, in fact, that it is now designated as its own country. God bless the USML.

JEFF'S NOTE: *My advice? Fry off a test sample! Before forming your loaf, take a tablespoon-size ball of the raw meat loaf and quickly sear it in a hot pan for a couple of minutes until no longer pink. Taste it! Does it need more salt? If so, add another 1 to 2 teaspoons of kosher salt to the mix and form.*

1 tablespoon olive oil
1 small yellow onion, cut into small dice
3 teaspoons kosher salt
3 garlic cloves, minced
2 large eggs
1 tablespoon Dijon mustard
1 tablespoon Worcestershire sauce
1 teaspoon hot sauce, such as Tabasco
½ cup whole milk
1 teaspoon freshly ground black pepper
1 pound ground chuck
½ pound ground pork
½ pound ground veal
1 cup coarsely crushed saltines
    (about 24 crackers)
⅓ cup minced flat-leaf parsley

GLAZE
½ cup sweet barbecue sauce
2 tablespoons sriracha
¼ cup packed dark brown sugar
¼ cup apple cider vinegar

1. Preheat the oven to 350°F. Line a rimmed medium or half-sheet pan with parchment paper.

2. Set a large skillet over medium heat. Add the oil and onion, sprinkle with 1 teaspoon of the kosher salt, and sauté the onion until translucent, 3 to 5 minutes. Add the garlic and sauté for 1 to 2 minutes, until fragrant and soft but not brown. Remove from the heat and set aside to cool.

3. Whisk the eggs, mustard, Worcestershire, hot sauce, milk, pepper, and the remaining 2 teaspoons salt in a large bowl. Add the meat, crackers, parsley, and onion-garlic mixture. Mix with your hands until evenly combined.

4. Turn the mixture onto the prepared sheet pan. Using your hands, gently form the meat mixture into a rustic loaf, about 9 × 5 inches.

5. To make the glaze, combine the barbecue sauce, sriracha, brown sugar, and vinegar in a small bowl. Slather half the glaze over the meat loaf, reserving the rest for basting.

6. Bake for about 1 hour (or until the meat loaf registers 165°F in the center), basting halfway through. Let rest for 20 minutes and serve. Store any leftovers in an airtight container in the fridge for up to 2 days.

'Cause there ain't
no doubt I love
this loaf . . .

That's how you do
leftover meat loaf.

Meat Loaf Sliders with Cheddar and Crispy Onions

MAKES 12 SLIDERS

This recipe was designed for leftover meat loaf. Sure, you can use fresh-from-the-oven meat loaf, but let's face it, leftover meat loaf is basically one of the founding pillars of our great country. You owe it to *your* family and *your* country to make sandwiches with leftover meat loaf.

Picture a bald eagle wearing blue jeans eating a cheeseburger while watching baseball (and keeping score) in camo socks and sipping a cold one out of a beer koozie. That's how American leftover meat loaf sandwiches are. Just do it.

⅓ recipe United States of Meat Loaf (page 78), chilled

1 cup shredded Cheddar (about 4 ounces)

One 12-count package sweet rolls (I like King's Hawaiian sweet rolls)

8 tablespoons (1 stick) salted butter, at room temperature, for griddling

½ cup meat loaf glaze (see page 78; optional)

½ cup sliced pickles (optional)

1 cup crispy onions

1. Adjust an oven rack to the middle position and preheat the oven to broil. Line a sheet pan with parchment paper.

2. Cut the *cold* leftover meat loaf into 1-inch-thick slices. Then slice into quarters.

3. Place the patties on the prepared sheet pan and cover each slice with a mound of cheese. Broil until the cheese is bubbly and starting to brown and the meat loaf is heated through.

4. As always, butter and griddle your bread! Set a large nonstick skillet over medium heat. Schmear butter on both insides of each bun and, working in batches, place butter side down on the skillet. Gently griddle until golden brown, about 5 minutes.

5. Place the meat loaf–cheese patties on the buns and top with meat loaf glaze and pickle slices, if using, and crispy onions—or just serve plain, because let's face it, most children eat things plain. Lorenzo loves stuff plain, explaining, "I really want to experience the flavors of the meat, cheese, and bread." Who am I to judge?

Lorenzo's Favorite Burger

MAKES 4 BURGERS

See photo on page 74.

My boy loves cheeseburgers but not all cheeseburgers. He has developed a discerning palate for this legendary combination of meat, cheese, and bread.

Lorenzo's criteria for great cheeseburgers are as follows:

1. Meat, cheese, and bread only; no garnish or setup
2. Cooked to medium—no more, no less
3. Salt, pepper, and beef only. No weird onion soup mix-ins or seasonings in the beef
4. Buttered and griddled bread
5. The cheese must be melted and gooey—no room-temp solid cheese product here
6. Don't cut the burger in half. Always eat it whole so the juice doesn't run out

What can I say? The kid is passionate about his burgers, and I fully support this passion.

2 pounds whole chuck roast, cut into 1-inch cubes
1 tablespoon kosher salt
1 teaspoon freshly ground black pepper
4 slices American cheese
4 tablespoons (½ stick) salted butter, at room temperature, for griddling
4 brioche buns

1. Place the beef chunks on a sheet pan in a single layer, leaving ½ inch of space around each chunk. Freeze the meat until very firm and starting to harden around edges but still pliable, 15 to 25 minutes.
2. Place half the meat in a food processor and pulse until coarsely ground, ten to fifteen 1-second pulses, stopping and redistributing the meat around the bowl as necessary to ensure the beef is evenly ground. Transfer the ground meat to the sheet pan by overturning the food processor bowl, without directly touching the meat. Repeat to grind the remaining meat.
3. Spread the meat over the sheet pan and inspect carefully, discarding any long strands of gristle or large chunks of hard meat or fat. Season each side with the salt and pepper.
4. Set a large cast-iron skillet or square flat-bottomed nonstick griddle pan (not a grill pan) over high heat.
5. Divide the meat into four portions and form large, thin patties with your hands. Make sure not to pack the meat too tightly. Working in batches, place the patties in the skillet and press down on them once with a spatula. Do not smoosh them again. After 4 to 5 minutes, when crusty brown, flip and place a slice of cheese on top of each patty. Cook for another 5 minutes, until crusty brown.
6. As always, butter and griddle your bread! Set a large nonstick skillet over medium heat. Schmear the butter on both insides of each bun and, working in batches, place butter side down on the skillet. Gently griddle until golden brown, about 5 minutes.
7. Place the burgers on the buns and serve immediately.

Crispy Broccoli with Asiago and Pine Nuts

MAKES 4 SERVINGS

The broccoli in this dish is saturated with lemon and funky Asiago flavor, yet the outside is crispy and charred. It's a ton of flavor using very few ingredients, and not only will your kids love it, but your whole family with begin to obsess over this broccoli dish.

¼ cup olive oil, plus ½ teaspoon for toasting the pine nuts
½ cup shredded Asiago (about 2 ounces)
½ teaspoon sugar
2 teaspoons kosher salt
1 teaspoon freshly ground black pepper
2 broccoli crowns, cut into 1½-inch florets (reserve the broccoli stems to use in Broccoli Stem "Fries," page 86)
¼ cup pine nuts
Zest and juice of 1 lemon

1. Preheat the oven to 400°F.
2. Combine the ¼ cup oil, cheese, sugar, salt, and pepper in a large bowl. Add the broccoli and toss to coat. Spread the broccoli in an even layer on a sheet pan and roast for 20 to 30 minutes, until the tops are slightly charred, stirring halfway through the roasting process.
3. Heat the remaining ½ teaspoon oil in a small skillet over medium-low heat. Add the pine nuts and gently toast, shaking the pan often, until lightly golden, 3 or 4 minutes. Pine nuts go from perfectly toasted to brutally burned in the amount of time it takes for you to call your mom, check the mail, or unload the dishwasher. It happens that quick, so be attentive and do not ever, under any circumstances, underestimate the toasting sensitivity of a tender pine nut.
4. Sprinkle the lemon zest and juice over the broccoli, toss, top with the pine nuts, and serve!

Broccoli Stem "Fries"

MAKES 4 SERVINGS

These fries make the most out of the whole stalk of broccoli. Don't toss out those delicious stems; instead, give them a new life in the form of a fry. Your kids will gobble these up and you'll sit back and smile, knowing they're eating vegetables while you are saving money, reducing waste, and single-handedly saving the planet with one of my clever recipes. Long live the Sandwich King!

8 broccoli stems
1 cup all-purpose flour
2 large eggs
1 cup bread crumbs
1 cup grated Parmigiano-Reggiano
   (about 4 ounces), plus more for garnish
Kosher salt and freshly ground black pepper
Vegetable oil cooking spray
1 cup Easiest Cheese Sauce of All Time
   (page 42) or your favorite store-bought

1. Preheat the oven to 400°F. Set a wire rack on a rimmed sheet pan.

2. Peel off the hard, woody exterior of the broccoli stems. Cut each stem in half lengthwise, then in half again lengthwise so it's quartered. Cut them across if necessary; "fries" should be 3 to 4 inches long.

3. Create a breading line with three separate large shallow bowls. Place the flour in the first bowl. In the second bowl, whisk the eggs with 2 tablespoons of water. In the third bowl, stir together the bread crumbs, cheese, salt, and pepper to combine. Working with one "fry" at a time, use one hand to dredge it in the flour, shaking off any excess. Use your other hand to dip the "fry" into the egg mixture, coating it completely. Use your dry hand to evenly coat the "fry" with the bread crumb mixture. Place it on the prepared wire rack. Repeat to bread the rest of the "fries."

4. Spray the "fries" with a light coating of vegetable oil cooking spray. Bake until golden brown, 20 to 25 minutes. Serve with your favorite cheese sauce. These go amazingly well with cheese—I mean, what doesn't?

Not a packet of
cheese powder in
sight . . .

Stovetop Ooey Gooey Mac and Cheese

MAKES 4 TO 6 SERVINGS

Remember when your mom would make boxed Kraft macaroni and cheese? She'd mix the hot pasta with the cold butter, the milk, and that packet of fluorescent cheese powder. It was audible from a distance, the sound of the spoon sloshing against the macaroni as it became one with the instant cheese sauce. I could not wait to dig in . . . at least for the first few minutes of its life.

To me, boxed mac and cheese lasts just a mere couple of minutes before it starts to seize up and lose its luxurious creaminess. That's why as a kid I would inhale my bowl of mac and cheese within three minutes, usually resulting in what my father called "agita."

This recipe extends those glorious first three minutes for an additional thirty minutes and beyond. I've cracked the code.

Kosher salt
1 pound fusilli pasta
2 cups freshly grated sharp Cheddar (about 8 ounces)
8 ounces Velveeta or similar foil-wrapped shelf-stable cheese stuff, cut into 1-inch cubes

2 tablespoons cornstarch
Two 12-ounce cans evaporated milk
2 teaspoons Dijon mustard
1 cup pulverized butter crackers, like Ritz

1. Bring a large pot of salted water to a boil. Add the pasta and cook until al dente according to the package instructions. Drain and return the pasta to the pot.
2. In a medium bowl toss the cheeses and cornstarch until the cheese is fully coated.
3. Set a medium saucepan over low heat. Add the evaporated milk and mustard and whisk until smooth. Whisk in the cheeses and cook, stirring constantly, for about 5 minutes, until all the cheese is melted and the sauce is silky and smooth.
4. Add the cheese sauce to the pasta and stir until you reach dream cheesiness. Serve in a bowl and top with pulverized crackers. Watch the children cry tears of happiness . . . and then realize that boxed mac and cheese will no longer be accepted.

The Sloppy Lo

MAKES 8 SANDWICHES

Lorenzo's nickname is Lo, or LoLo. Like all great nicknames, its origin is entirely organic and really unexplainable. We didn't choose Lo; Lo chose him. You would think people would call him Enzo or Zo, but those never stuck. Lo has a great ring to it, and since I named this recipe after his nickname, he is forever dubbed Lo . . . at least in his old man's eyes.

2 teaspoons olive oil
2 pounds ground turkey or ground sirloin
½ medium yellow onion, cut into small dice
2 celery stalks, cut into small dice
2 small carrots, grated
1 cup ketchup
Two 8-ounce cans tomato sauce
1 tablespoon packed light brown sugar
2 tablespoons apple cider vinegar
1 teaspoon kosher salt
¼ teaspoon freshly ground black pepper
4 tablespoons (½ stick) salted butter, at room
   temperature, for griddling
8 whole wheat buns
1 recipe Pickled Cukes and Carrots (page 69)

1. Heat 1 teaspoon of the oil in a large skillet over medium heat. Add the turkey and brown until no longer pink, breaking it up as it cooks. Set aside in a medium bowl. Add the remaining 1 teaspoon oil and the onion, celery, and carrots and sauté until softened, about 10 minutes. Return the turkey to the skillet and add the ketchup, tomato sauce, brown sugar, vinegar, salt, and pepper. Simmer until thickened, about 15 minutes.

2. As always, butter and griddle your bread! Set a large nonstick skillet over medium heat. Schmear butter on both insides of each bun and, working in batches, place butter side down on the skillet. Gently griddle until golden brown, about 5 minutes.

3. Scoop the Sloppy Lo mix onto the buns and top with pickles. Serve with 14 napkins, preferably near a bathtub or garden hose.

"Hoagies and grinders,
hoagies and grinders . . .
navy beans, navy beans . . .
meatloaf sandwich . . ."
—Adam Sandler

In my neighborhood we call that a "quad stack."

Jalapeño Popper Grilled Cheese

MAKES 4 SANDWICHES

This has all the flavor of your favorite sampler platter but in grilled cheese form!

6 whole jalapeños
1 tablespoon olive oil
½ teaspoon kosher salt
¼ teaspoon freshly ground black pepper
8 thick slices country white bread
4 tablespoons (½ stick) unsalted butter,
    at room temperature
½ cup mascarpone or full-fat cream cheese
1 cup shredded aged Cheddar
    (about 4 ounces)
Tortilla chips (optional)

1. Adjust an oven rack to the middle position and preheat the oven to broil. Line a sheet pan with parchment paper.

2. Toss the jalapeños with the oil, salt, and pepper in a medium bowl. Lay them on the prepared sheet pan and broil for 8 minutes, turning once, until the skin is blistered. Place the peppers in a plastic bag and let sit for a few minutes to let the skin loosen. Using a paper towel, gently pull off the charred and blistered skin. Halve each jalapeño and remove the majority of seeds and ribs. If you want your sandwich blazingly hot, keep the seeds and ribs! Set aside.

3. Spread the butter on one side of each of the bread slices, crust to crust. This ensures even griddling without burning all that precious butter. Remember, it's a lot easier to butter the bread *before* you build!

4. In a medium bowl, combine the cheeses using a rubber spatula. Spread the mixture evenly on each of the unbuttered sides of the bread slices. Place sliced jalapeños on 4 of the bread slices and top with the remaining bread slices, butter side out, nestling the peppers within the cheese.

5. Set a large heavy griddle pan (not a grill pan) or a square flat-bottomed 12-inch nonstick skillet over medium-low heat. Place the sandwiches on the griddle and "dome" them with a large metal bowl or skillet lid to create a heat vortex to ensure maximum interior meltitude. Cook for about 5 minutes, or until golden brown, and then flip and repeat until the interior is gooey and both sides are golden brown, another 5 minutes. For extra credit, sneak some crispy tortilla chips into the sandwich to give it some extra crunch!

6. Cut each sandwich in half and bask in the glory of this amazing creation that I've single-handedly provided for you and your closest loved ones.

The Most Perfect Grilled Cheese

MAKES 4 SANDWICHES

Grilled cheese, or as Lorenzo calls it, "grillcheese," should never be rushed. The lower and slower you go, the better the meltitude of the American cheese and the more golden and evenly crisped the exterior. After years or decades of attempts, I can promise you that when peak grilled cheese is finally achieved, the heavens will open, the angels will weep tears of elation, and you will forever be bathed in the warm bright light of transcendence. And that's a Jeff Mauro Guarantee.

JEFF MAURO'S PRO TIP: *Get the good American cheese, sliced to order from the deli. It makes a world of difference. It tastes better and melts better; plus, if you're friendly enough, they usually let you sample the first slice.*

8 thick slices country white bread
20 slices deli American cheese
8 tablespoons (1 stick) salted butter, at room temperature

1. Spread butter on one side of each of the bread slices, crust to crust. This ensures even griddling without burning all that precious butter. Remember, it's a lot easier to butter the bread *before* you build!

2. Set a large heavy griddle pan (not a grill pan) or a square flat-bottomed 12-inch nonstick skillet over medium-low heat.

3. For each sandwich, lay 5 cheese slices in between 2 bread slices, covering thickly and completely.*

4. Working in batches as needed, place the sandwiches on the griddle and "dome" them with a large metal bowl or skillet lid to create a proper vortex of heat. Cook for about 5 minutes, or until golden brown, then flip and repeat until the interior is gooey and both sides are golden brown, another 5 minutes.

5. Cut the sandwiches and watch the cascade of gooey good ol' American cheese catch the sunlight streaming through the kitchen window and throw a glow of warm orange light throughout your entire house.

---

* *I know this sounds excessive, but it ensures the most possible ooey gooeyness. You can scale back to 3 slices if 5 slices are too many for whatever reason.*

Look at the "faccia"!

. . . and that Class 7 cheese pull.

5

DO YOU SMELL THAT MEAT SMOKE? THAT'S RIGHT, IT'S COMING FROM MY BACKYARD

The last sentence on my professional, self-written bio is: "My favorite color is pastrami and my favorite smell is meat smoke." Meat cooked outdoors over smoldering natural wood is ethereal, and I defy anyone walking past my home while I'm in the throes of a smoke session to not instantly rethink their dinner plans.

Jeff's BBQ and Smoking Tips

1. If you don't have a dedicated smoker, get yourself a smoker box on Amazon. They are cheap, effective, and the best way to achieve a low and slow smoke on a gas grill.

2. If you don't have a smoker box, fashion yourself a smoker packet using two layers of aluminum foil and a couple of cups of wood chips (they come in all sorts of varieties like hickory, apple, cherry, and oak—just check the bag to make sure they are for smoking, not for landscaping or mulching!). Flatten it out into a 10 × 5-inch packet, poke some holes in the top, and place it over low flame until smoking. Have a spray bottle full of water to tame the flame once it ignites. Also, you can put chips directly in a small disposable aluminum tray and place it directly on the burner until smoking. I prefer spraying water on the chips post-smoking to help slow it down. If you soak the chips ahead of time, it takes too long to get them smoking. Which reminds me . . .

3. Be patient. Other than wrapping your meat in foil or peach/butcher paper toward the end of your cook, you really can't rush the process.

4. Peach or butcher paper is better than foil for wrapping your meat. Though foil will accelerate the cooking process more, peach or butcher paper will preserve the bark more. Head to Amazon and purchase a roll that will last you many summers to come.

5. Use a good digital instant-read thermometer. Please. Aren't we all there yet? Thermapen makes the best one, and mine has lasted me sixteen years. Smoking meat is a game of Fahrenheits and feel. Time is just a guideline, but the temperature of the inside of the meat rarely disappoints. The Goldilocks zone of smoked meats is 200°F to 203°F.

6. When doing long cooks like beef ribs, pork ribs, pork shoulder, or brisket, place a small metal bowl or disposable aluminum tray filled with warm water directly on the grates. This helps maintain the moist environment that contributes to moist meat.

7. Crack a beer and consume at least 1.5 beers per hour of your cook. Stop at six beers, though—you don't want to get too loaded and miss those crucial temps.

8. Smoked meat rests well. Please don't wait to put your long-cook meat on the smoker until just a few minutes before your guests arrive. Have it ready and rested or just about to finish and rest. You don't want people waiting around the smoker at midnight, starving and hangry. You'll have a mutiny on your hands and no one will ever come over again.

9. Get yourself a dedicated cooler to rest that meat in. Magic happens when your smoked meat is wrapped and rested in a controlled environment such as a cooler. Use it to your advantage, especially when trying to time a reasonable mealtime.

10. Vacuum seal and freeze any leftover meat that you know you won't eat the next day. When it's time to reheat, heat a pot of water to 167°F (use that thermometer!) and place the vacuum-sealed bag directly in the water and gently heat for about 30 minutes. This is a wonderful way to preserve all that succulence and smoke without drying it out in the microwave (NO!!!!!) or hot oven.

Smoked BBQ Cheddar Crackers

MAKES 4 SERVINGS

These are by far the easiest things in the world to smoke. There is no rendering of fats, no constant temperature taking or babysitting, but the results are ridiculously addictive. Play around with different types of crackers: butter crackers, saltines, oyster crackers, even croutons! Such a great appetizer or make-ahead snack to get your family's and guests' mouths pining for more smoky goodness!

EQUIPMENT: smoker, grill with a smoker box, or grill with a hickory wood chip packet

One 21-ounce box Cheez-Its
Vegetable oil cooking spray

¼ cup The Best All-Purpose BBQ Rub (page 35)
1 cup ranch dressing (see page 127)

1. Preheat the smoker to 225°F using hickory wood chips.
2. Place the Cheez-Its in a disposable aluminum pan. Spray all the Cheez-Its with cooking spray and coat in the rub. Place on the smoker and smoke away for 1 hour, stirring once at 30 minutes. (Remember, *if you lookin', you ain't cookin'!*)
3. Serve warm in a bowl with a side of my famous ranch dressing or your favorite sauce for dipping.

Chicken thighs:
the bacon of
the sky

Chicken Shawarma Wrap

MAKES 4 SERVINGS

The first time I had shawarma was on a college trip to Europe when I was twenty. We were a group of thirty kids traveling with our professors from Bradley University to various European cities, where we would take daily classes on various subjects (theater in London, biology in Austria, journal writing in Malta) in exchange for college credits. Truth be told, it was a racket. We would learn for a couple hours a day, do a little homework, and then party late into the night. Best nine credits ever.

Anyway, being college students and all, me and my buddies Leno, Brad, and Jason decided to go rogue one free weekend and take a quick puddle jumper from London to Amsterdam. We were eager to experience the famous Dutch café culture.

We landed, took a train downtown, and ended up renting a cheap room from a shady, well-dressed Turkish fella standing under an open umbrella next to a phone booth outside the train station. In a residential neighborhood filled with never-ending blocks of identical row houses, the room was a bit off the grid. Basic essentials were covered, with four bunks, a TV, a bathroom, and a stinky kitchen, which I immediately inspected and found a funky half of an old onion omelet sitting in a skillet on the stove. Not being one for food smells where I sleep, I promptly opened the kitchen window and threw that thing outside.

We quickly dropped our bags off and hit the town to experience our first-ever real-deal Amsterdam café. We walked the town for a bit and settled on the first café that we encountered. For the next two hours, we made ourselves at home indulging in strong coffee and even stronger pot.

After hitting our limit, we decided to go back to our room, get cleaned up, and find us some dinner. We started walking, more like floating, down the miles of row houses, our stomachs all growling and ready for our first real meal of the day. We were tired yet elated at the adventure. Finally, one us spoke up: "Hey, anyone remember where we are staying?" Which was followed by a four-pack of stoned blank stares.

Truth was, all we had was a single key. Nothing with an address. Not one of us knew the cross streets or even the actual name of our street. Remember, these are all blocks and blocks of row houses on streets with very Dutch names. Keizersgracht, Lindenstraat. *Spaarndammerplantsoen*. Whatever recollections we had were left at the café.

We were lost, very paranoid, and extremely hungry. A terrible combination, especially while in a foreign country without our passports in pre–cell phone civilization. Our passports were "safely locked up" in our onion-scented flat rented from a mustachioed Turkish chap outside the train station. On top of that, our professors and parents had *zero* knowledge of our whereabouts because we thought it was cooler to take on this adventure without the wisdom and advice of our perhaps nay-saying elders.

It was a bad scene: four hippie-ish Americans aimlessly wandering down streets, arguing and cursing while trying to fit a blank key into a bunch of random front doors.

"Brad, you're the map guy! What the hell!"
"Leno, quit laughing, this is not funny, we are so damn screwed. We're going to be *detained, quarantined, and deported!*" "I want my mom." "Dear Lord, if you get us out of this, I will dedicate my life to the cloth . . ."

For more than three hours, we frantically searched for our apartment. Being a lifelong catastrophist, for those three hours I visited and revisited the many stages of grief. I finally came to the acceptance that this was the end. For all of us. I would be living the rest of my days here in this cruel city as a hardworking yet underpaid Dutch dishwasher. This was it. The end. *Stop trying that stupid key in every stupid door. It doesn't fit. I told you guys we should've told the professors! I'm scared. I'm hungry. I'm thirsty! Stupid. Stupid. STUPID!*

That's it. I gave up and was about to go confess to a nearby *politie* when I looked down, and right at my feet, lying on the sidewalk right up against the front door of a cookie-cutter pale blond row home, was an onion omelet. Half an onion omelet, to be precise. Right side up and intact, and welcoming us to the only home we'd known in Amsterdam.

"Brad, try the key."

Needless to say, we lived. That night we celebrated into the wee hours, drinking and laughing. We punctuated the evening outside a bar at a crowded shawarma cart. I'll never forget the flavor and feeling of those fluffy pitas, stuffed with vertically broiled chicken shawarma, fresh veggies, and liters of creamy tahini, all dosed in pungent hot sauce. The four of us ate like sultans and toasted our Heinekens to the fact that on this day we went rogue, almost died, and were saved by an omelet.

EQUIPMENT: smoker, grill with a smoker box, or grill with a mesquite wood chip packet

¼ cup olive oil
Zest and juice of 2 lemons
3 garlic cloves, smashed and roughly chopped
1 teaspoon kosher salt
1 teaspoon ground cumin
1 teaspoon sweet paprika
¼ teaspoon ground allspice
¼ teaspoon chili powder
⅛ teaspoon ground cinnamon
½ teaspoon ground turmeric
6 skin-on, bone-in chicken thighs
Vegetable oil, for greasing
1 recipe Tomato-Cucumber Relish (recipe follows), for serving
Dreamy Creamy Tahini (opposite), for serving
Fluffy pita, for serving

1. Whisk the olive oil, lemon zest and juice, garlic, salt, cumin, paprika, allspice, chili powder, cinnamon, and turmeric in a medium bowl. Reserve half the marinade for serving—this stuff is pure love!

2. Add the chicken to the bowl, mix to coat with the marinade, cover, and marinate in the fridge for at least 2 hours but up to 12 hours (the longer, the better).

3. Soak 1 cup of mesquite wood chips in water for 10 minutes. Place the packet (see page 98) directly on the burner and set all burners to high until smoking. Reduce the heat on two of the four burners and check the temperature; you're looking for it to register 375°F. Oil the grill grates with the vegetable oil. Using indirect grilling (one hot side, one cool side), place the chicken skin side up on the cooler side of the grill and close the lid. Grill for

30 to 35 minutes, rotating the thighs every 5 or 6 minutes to help them cook evenly, until they register 165°F.

4. Adjust an oven rack to the middle position and preheat the oven to broil. Place the thighs on a sheet pan and broil until crispy and golden brown, about 5 minutes. This is way easier, cleaner, and more consistent than grilling them skin side down, which causes too many flare-ups and lost, torn skin.

5. Serve with the reserved marinade, relish, tahini, and some warm pita bread! Yes! Store any leftover chicken in an airtight container in the fridge for up to 2 days.

Tomato-Cucumber Relish

MAKES ABOUT 2 CUPS

2 Roma tomatoes, cut into small dice
1 English cucumber, cut into small dice
½ small red onion, minced
1 garlic clove, grated
2 tablespoons extra virgin olive oil
2 teaspoons apple cider vinegar or white balsamic vinegar
Juice of 1 lemon
1 teaspoon dried oregano
Handful of chopped fresh flat-leaf parsley
Kosher salt and freshly ground black pepper

Toss all the ingredients in a large bowl and adjust the seasonings as desired. Cover and let sit for at least 1 hour to marry the flavors.

Dreamy Creamy Tahini Sauce

MAKES ABOUT 2 CUPS

1 cup tahini
1 cup whole milk Greek yogurt
2 tablespoons extra virgin olive oil
Zest and juice of 1 lemon, more to taste
Kosher salt

Whisk the tahini, yogurt, oil, lemon zest and juice, and ½ cup water in a medium bowl. Thin out with more water or lemon juice if necessary. Season with salt to taste. Store in the fridge in an airtight container for up to 1 week.

Cedar plank salmon:
the bacon of the sea

Smoked Honey-Glazed Cedar Plank Salmon

MAKES 4 TO 6 SERVINGS

This is a family favorite, especially for holidays. It feeds a bunch of fish to a bunch of people with minimal preparation and zero fish flipping. It's simple to cook to the desired temperature. The aroma of the cedar penetrates every bit of rich salmon and the sweetness really comes of age in the smoker.

EQUIPMENT: one 18-inch cedar plank; smoker, grill with a smoker box, or grill with an applewood or cherrywood chip packet

½ cup honey
2 tablespoons soy sauce
2 tablespoons apple cider vinegar
1 teaspoon red pepper flakes
One 1½- to 2-pound side skin-on salmon
1 tablespoon kosher salt

1. Soak the cedar plank in water for 2 hours.
2. Whisk the honey, soy sauce, vinegar, and red pepper flakes in a small bowl. Reserve about a quarter of the glaze for final basting once the salmon is cooked.
3. Place the salmon skin side down on the soaked plank. Brush a liberal amount of the honey glaze on the salmon. Season with the salt. Let the salmon chill out in the fridge for 1 hour to quick cure. This will tighten things up and keep the "white stuff" (albumin) from coming through in the smoked fish.
4. Preheat the smoker to 250°F using your wood chips of choice.
5. Once the smoke is going, place the cedar plank directly on the grates and go low and slow, basting every 15 minutes, until the internal temp registers 125°F for medium-rare, 130°F for medium, or 135°F for medium-well, about 40 to 60 minutes.
6. Hit the salmon with the reserved glaze before serving!

Reverse-Seared Rib Eyes

MAKES 4 TO 6 SERVINGS

For good reason, this method is the new standard for large-format steaks. It's foolproof and super controllable. What remains is a perfectly cooked steak, evenly medium or medium-rare from top to bottom, without that unpleasant band of overcooked gray meat. It's so darn easy, too, and you still get to sear some steak hard. Don't neglect salting and drying the steak overnight. It really promotes caramelization, ensures full top-to-bottom seasoning, and helps make the meat more tender.

COWBOY TIP: *No need to rest the meat after searing. The steaks essentially rested that whole*

time they were in the oven. After you sear, slice and serve!

2 giant 1-pound bone-in rib eyes, the thicker the better
Kosher salt and freshly ground black pepper
1 tablespoon grapeseed oil
4 tablespoons (½ stick) unsalted butter

1. The night before cooking, remove these bad boys from the butcher paper and pat them dry with a paper towel. Sprinkle salt over both sides. Place them on a wire rack on a sheet pan and put them in the refrigerator, uncovered.

continues

I love the slightly pink hue the smoke brings to the party.

Let sit overnight. This ensures maximum dehydration on the surface of the steak, which pretty much guarantees a gratifying crust. It also gives the steak a more tender and well-seasoned interior. Everybody wins. Just do it. Geez . . .

2. Preheat the oven to 225°F.

3. Season all sides of the rib eyes liberally with pepper and place back on the same sheet pan you had in the fridge. Roast for 30 to 40 minutes, until 10 degrees below your desired internal temperature is reached (115°F for medium-rare, 125°F for medium). Remember, we still have to sear these bad boys, so the temp will increase about 10 degrees. Tent with foil and set aside.

4. Set a grill pan or large cast-iron skillet over high heat. Depending on the size of your steaks, you may have to work in two batches. Add the oil, then sear the steaks on one side for 1 or 2 minutes, until brown. Add the butter, flip the steaks, and sear the other side until brown, 1 or 2 minutes, basting with the melted butter the whole time. Hold the steak on its side, rotating as necessary, to sear the edges until beautifully browned.

5. Slice the bones off and cut the rib eyes into half-inch slices. I love separating the collar or cap (steak scientists call it the "spinalis") from the rib "eye." The collar is the thin strip of muscle that runs along the top of the rib eye; it's often prized as the most delectable cut, so highlight it! Serve immediately.

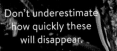

Don't underestimate how quickly these will disappear.

Honey-Glazed Pork Belly Burnt Ends

MAKES 6 TO 8 SERVINGS

If you take your time with this dish and really render that fat at a low and slow pace, you will achieve BBQ enlightenment. When you finally open the smoker or grill for the last time, you'll be greeted by a meat so darn shiny and reflective that it burns sun spots into your retinas. When you take your first scalding bite (because no person on the planet has the patience to wait), your taste buds are instantly inundated with ultra-caramelized crispy rendered pork fat followed by a monsoon of succulent and smoky swine. You'll make these once, you'll figure it out, you'll make them twice, you'll perfect them. It's that easy and the next thing you know, you'll be serving this dish at every party and bringing it to every get-together until the end of your wonderful, pork-filled life.

EQUIPMENT: smoker with cherrywood, applewood, or hickory wood

One 6- to 8-pound pork belly, skin removed if desired
2 tablespoons vegetable oil
¼ cup The Best All-Purpose BBQ Rub (page 35)
¼ cup packed dark brown sugar
8 tablespoons (1 stick) unsalted butter
1 cup BBQ sauce
3 tablespoons apple cider vinegar
¼ cup apple juice
1 tablespoon hot sauce, such as Cholula
3 tablespoons honey

continues

1. Preheat the smoker to 250°F using your wood chips of choice.

2. Cut the pork belly into 2-inch cubes. Toss them with the oil and BBQ rub in a large bowl. Spread the cubes evenly on a wire rack, fat side down, with about ½ inch of space between the cubes.

3. Place the rack directly on the grates of the smoker or grill and cook for 2 hours, until the pork is a deep mahogany color.

4. Place the smoked pork cubes snugly into a 9 × 13 aluminum pan. Sprinkle the brown sugar and butter all over the pork belly. Cover the pan in aluminum foil and return to the smoker for 1½ to 2 hours, until super tender and the interior of the meat registers 200°F.

5. To make the glaze, whisk the BBQ sauce, vinegar, apple juice, hot sauce, and honey in a medium bowl.

6. Drench the pork in the BBQ glaze and place back in the smoker for another 5 to 10 minutes, until super caramelized. I love serving these guys right in the aluminum pan with a bunch of toothpicks. It makes an unforgettable amuse-boosh [sic] that will have your guests obeying your every command for the next 2 to 3 months.

Smoked Cauliflower "Butt"

MAKES 4 SERVINGS

This took me many tries to perfect. The first key is poaching the cauliflower in salted and slightly vinegary water so that every fiber of the vegetable is totally seasoned. The other key is to baste frequently in your favorite sweet, spicy, or mustardy BBQ sauce. The goal is to have this big beautiful head of cauliflower shellacked in layer after layer of BBQ sauce.

EQUIPMENT: smoker, grill with a smoker box, or grill with an applewood or cherrywood chip packet

1 cup white vinegar
1 tablespoon kosher salt
1 head cauliflower, leaves removed and stem cut flush against florets to make a flat and stable base
2 cups BBQ sauce

1. Preheat the smoker to 300°F using your wood chips of choice.

2. Combine the vinegar, salt, and 3 cups water in a large saucepan. Place the cauliflower in the pot, cover, and bring to a gentle simmer over medium heat. Poach the cauliflower for 10 to 15 minutes, until par-cooked and not quite knife tender. You still want some resistance; it will finish on the smoker.

3. Drain the cauliflower and brush it with a liberal amount of BBQ sauce. Smoke for 1 hour, basting frequently with plenty of BBQ sauce, until knife tender and super caramelized with the hue of a red Italian leather armchair in a high-priced lawyer's office.

I am 100 percent
vegetarian.

Liquid Gold Honey-Mustard Sauce

MAKES ABOUT 3 CUPS

The vanilla is the secret to this Carolina-inspired mustard sauce. Trust me, don't skip it—it adds a subtle floral note that pairs well with the tangy mustard and sweet honey. This goes on *everything*: grilled chicken, smoked meats of any variety . . . try it in your favorite dressing or vinaigrette. Mix with mayo and a little buttermilk and you have the creamiest honey-mustard dressing.

1½ cups yellow mustard
½ cup apple cider vinegar
¼ cup honey
2 teaspoons Worcestershire sauce
1 teaspoon vanilla bean paste or pure vanilla extract
¼ cup packed light brown sugar
2 teaspoons hot sauce, such as Cholula
1 teaspoon freshly ground black pepper

Combine all the ingredients in a small saucepan over medium-high heat and bring to a simmer, whisking constantly. Simmer for 5 minutes, until the brown sugar is dissolved. Store in an airtight container in the fridge for up to 3 weeks.

Pastrami Rub Short Ribs

MAKES 6 TO 8 SERVINGS

People constantly ask what my favorite sandwich is. My answer depends on my current mood, but I often say a pastrami on rye with a schmear of Dijon mustard. I'm talking good house-made, hand-cut smoky pastrami covered in a peppery bark. This dish has all those flavors, but in non-sandwich form.

Like I always say, my favorite smell is meat smoke, and my favorite color . . . is pastrami.

RIB TIPS: *Make sure you allow enough time to let the short ribs marinate in the pastrami rub. Overnight is ideal, but it should be at least 8 hours. This really lets that flavor penetrate the meat and helps create a delectable bark. Also, be sure to make your pickled red cabbage ahead of time. It will get super funky and super pink with an overnight soak.*

EQUIPMENT: smoker, grill with a smoker box, or grill with an oak or hickory wood chip packet

¼ cup fresh coarsely ground black pepper
1 tablespoon kosher salt
1 tablespoon light brown sugar
2 tablespoons ground coriander
1 teaspoon mustard powder
1 tablespoon smoked paprika
2 teaspoons garlic powder

2 teaspoons onion powder
3 pounds English-cut short ribs
Liquid Gold Honey-Mustard Sauce (opposite), for serving
1 recipe Pickled Red Cabbage (recipe follows on page 118), for serving

1. Combine the pepper, salt, brown sugar, coriander, mustard powder, paprika, garlic powder, and onion powder in a small bowl.
2. Place the ribs on a medium sheet pan and rub thoroughly with the spice mixture. Cover the sheet pan in plastic wrap and let sit in the fridge overnight, or at least 8 hours.

continues

Legit smoke ring

3. Preheat a smoker with a water pan to 225°F using your wood chips of choice. Once your smoke is going, place the short ribs directly on the grates, bone side down. Smoke the ribs for 3 hours, or until the thickest part of the rib meat registers at 170°F. Wrap all the ribs in one even layer of peach paper or foil and put back on the smoker for another hour or so, or until the internal temperature hits 200°F. This helps accelerate the cooking process and ensures all that beautiful beef fat and collagen renders, leaving you with very tender beef ribs. Let the wrapped ribs rest for at least 1 hour before serving. This will keep all that rendered fat and collagen in the ribs, not on your cutting board.
4. Serve with the honey mustard and a side of pickled cabbage.

Pickled Red Cabbage

MAKES 1 QUART

I always say there are not enough purple foods, and pickled red cabbage is the most purpliest food.

1 cup white vinegar
2 tablespoons sugar
2 tablespoons kosher salt
½ head of a large red cabbage, sliced thin

1. Combine the vinegar, sugar, salt, and ½ cup water in a small saucepan over medium heat. Simmer until the sugar and salt have dissolved and remove from the heat.
2. Place the cabbage in a large bowl and add the warm pickling liquid. Let sit in an airtight container overnight in the fridge.

Now that's some
colorful BBQ.

Bluish steel

6

IT'S BEEN A LONG WEEKEND . . . GOTTA DETOX . . . WE'RE COOKING HEALTHY

The inset photo opposite (big orange) was taken as I was starting my health and fitness journey about seven years ago. Part of me wanted to feel better and perform better. A fair amount of me wanted to look better on-screen. They say the camera adds fifteen pounds; well, in my case it added about thirty-eight pounds (thanks, 4K TV!), which was personally hard to watch. You see, I run "chubby," and it took many years to figure out what works for me to stay on target and feel good. It all starts in the kitchen and what you put in your body. Fitness is important, but diet is crucial, and I've found that if I really focus on well-balanced and colorful meals 80 percent of the time, I can get a little naughty and indulgent for the remaining 20 percent. I love food too damn much to go the full 100 percent. Sarah is a full 100 percenter, and she is an absolute specimen of inspiration. This chapter is dedicated to her. For many reasons, including our diet, she keeps us all very healthy and happy.

Rainbow Crudité and Cinnamon Hummus

MAKES ABOUT 2 CUPS

I'm not a huge believer in serving an overwhelming number of appetizers. Guests tend to overindulge in chips, dips, charcuterie, and cheese-and-salami-stuffed dough balls, and when the time comes for the main event, they have nothing left in the tank. Their appetites have been strangled by a cornucopia of too many damn apps, and that special main course you spent so much energy prepping and preparing is just not as exciting. I want people *very hungry* when dinner is served.

That's why crudité of well-cut and colorful vegetables always does the trick. It takes the edge off your guests' hunger without stuffing their tummies with a much-too-tempting selection of salty meat, gooey cheese, and crusty bread. Veggies are healthy and crunchy and hummus is creamy and slightly indulgent. It scratches the itch without breaking the skin . . . ya know what I mean?

Serve with apples, peppers of all colors, carrots, and celery, or just eat it like it is. Trust me, you'll love it!

One 15-ounce can chickpeas, drained and
    rinsed
¼ cup smooth peanut butter
¼ cup pure maple syrup
1½ teaspoons ground cinnamon
1 teaspoon pure vanilla extract
2 tablespoons apple cider vinegar
¼ teaspoon sea salt

Place all the ingredients in the bowl of a food processor and blend until smooth. Adjust the consistency with 1 teaspoon of water at a time until the mixture is at your desired consistency. Make sure there are no chunks of chickpeas remaining. Store in an airtight container in the fridge for up to 1 week.

A CLEVER TRAY OF CRUDITÉ

When assembling crudité, it is important to build with color and texture. Here are my favorite crudité components:

RAINBOW CARROTS: green leafy tops trimmed slightly and peeled to a dramatic bullet-like point

GREEN BEANS: trimmed green beans, blanched in a large pot of salted boiling water and quickly dunked in ice water until chilled, then drained

SNAP PEAS: same as above; just make sure you remove those tough little "strings" before blanching

WATERMELON RADISHES: raw and sliced into half-moons; they're a beautiful pink color and there is definitely not enough pink food

SMALL RED RADISHES: cleaned and used whole, with a little green top still intact

ENGLISH CUCUMBERS: sliced into spears so you can get a handle on them

MINI MULTICOLORED BELL PEPPERS: sliced in half, so you can get a nice swipe of dip on the inside

BROCCOLI AND CAULIFLOWER: served trimmed and raw or blanched, shocked, and drained, which brightens them up and tones down their texture

The sleeper hit of the cookbook

Crispy Shaved Brussels Sprout Salad with Mandarin Oranges

MAKES 4 SERVINGS

I have a soft spot for salads you can eat with a spoon. This here salad is totally and gratifyingly spoonable. Unfortunately, the world has yet to invent a salad spoon. I'll get right on it.

Two 16-ounce bags shaved Brussels sprouts
¼ cup plus 2 tablespoons olive oil
Kosher salt and freshly ground black pepper
½ cup slivered almonds
2 tablespoons rice wine vinegar
2 tablespoons Dijon mustard
2 green onions, thinly sliced on the bias, white and green parts separated
One 10-ounce can mandarin oranges
½ cup crunchy wonton strips

1. Preheat the oven to 400°F. Line two rimmed sheet pans with parchment paper.
2. In a large bowl, toss the sprouts with the 2 tablespoons oil and season with salt and pepper. Spread them evenly on the prepared sheet pans and roast, stirring halfway through, until the sprouts are beginning to brown and crisp around the edges, about 20 minutes. Let cool slightly.
3. Set a small skillet over medium-low heat. Add the almonds and toast, stirring frequently, until a nutty aroma fills the air and the color has darkened a bit, about 8 minutes.
4. Meanwhile, whisk the vinegar, mustard, and the green onion whites in a large bowl. Slowly pour in the remaining ¼ cup oil and whisk until emulsified. Add salt and pepper to taste.
5. When ready to serve, add the sprouts, mandarin oranges, and almonds to the dressing and gently toss to combine. Taste and adjust the seasoning. Pile high on a serving platter and top with the wonton strips and the reserved green onion greens.

100 percent spoonable salad

Chopped Cobb Salad with Ranch Dressing

MAKES 4 TO 6 SERVINGS

This salad resides in the healthy chapter because, technically, the Cobb salad is a salad. Let's face it, though, this is the original complete stand-alone salad meal. It contains 89 percent of all known ingredients in the world and will leave your belly full to the brim every time. Especially when served with some warm crusty bread.

WHEN I TIP, YOU TIP, WE TIP: *This is the best ranch dressing you will ever have. Make a bunch of it, coat every green in it, and dunk every nugget in it. It gets better the longer it chills. Also, traditional Cobb salads include chunks of deli turkey or grilled chicken, so feel free to bulk yours up with those items or some leftover rotisserie chicken.*

RANCH DRESSING

½ cup mayonnaise

¼ cup sour cream

2 tablespoons fresh lemon juice

1 teaspoon dried dill

1 teaspoon dried parsley

½ teaspoon garlic powder

½ teaspoon onion powder

1 teaspoon kosher salt

½ teaspoon freshly ground black pepper

Up to ¼ cup heavy (whipping) cream

SALAD

4 cups roughly chopped romaine lettuce

10 bacon slices, cooked using the Mauro Method (see page 19), roughly chopped

1 small red onion, cut into small dice

2 avocados, pitted, peeled, and cut into ¾-inch dice

¾ cup cherry tomatoes, sliced in half

½ cup blue cheese crumbles

1. To make the dressing, whisk the mayo, sour cream, lemon juice, dill, parsley, garlic powder, onion powder, salt, and pepper in a medium bowl. Add the cream a bit at a time until the dressing reaches the consistency you like. I like mine a little looser so it evenly coats the entire salad. Place in your favorite serving dish and set aside until ready to serve.

2. To assemble the salad, use a serving bowl that you find special and get creative. I like to put the lettuce on the bottom and make little rows of bacon, onion, avocado, and tomatoes on top and then sprinkle blue cheese over everything, but this is *your* salad. Build it how you like. Serve the salad with the dressing on the side.

Portobello Bacon

You 100 percent will make this more than once and make it often. Good luck not eating it all before it makes it to the table. Dare I say, it's almost better than bacon. That's not hyperbole, either. Portobello bacon is just as addictive and much better for you. That being said, nothing beats pig bacon.

2 tablespoons olive oil

2 tablespoons soy sauce

1 tablespoon rice vinegar

2 large portobello mushrooms, stems and gills removed, cut into ¼-inch slices

1 teaspoon granulated garlic

½ teaspoon smoked paprika

1 tablespoon light brown sugar

1 teaspoon kosher salt

1. Preheat the oven to 400°F. Place a wire rack on a rimmed sheet pan.

2. Whisk the oil, soy sauce, and vinegar in a large bowl, then add the mushrooms and coat.

3. Place the mushrooms on the prepared sheet pan and sprinkle with the granulated garlic, paprika, brown sugar, and salt.

4. Bake for 15 to 20 minutes, until deep golden brown. Let cool for 15 minutes. The mushrooms will crisp up as they cool and get even more "bacony." After they've rested, eat immediately because they don't keep very well. They are so addictive that you'll plow through them in minutes.

Grilled Greek Summer Salad

MAKES 4 TO 6 SERVINGS

We grew up going only to Italian restaurants or restaurants in Greek Town, usually on Saturday night or after Sunday mass. This salad reminds me of the big salads we would share at our usual Greek Town haunts—Roditys, Athena, and Pegasus. Tons of crisp romaine was doused in vinegar and topped with planks and planks of salty feta. The flash grilling of the romaine adds a fun modern spin and smoky edge to this classic salad.

SWEET GREEK DRESSING

½ cup red wine vinegar

1 garlic clove, minced or grated with a
Microplane

2 tablespoons honey

1 teaspoon dried oregano

1 teaspoon Dijon mustard

Kosher salt and freshly ground black pepper

½ cup olive oil

SALAD

Four 6-ounce boneless, skinless chicken breast
halves, patted dry

Vegetable oil, for greasing

2 romaine lettuce hearts, halved but with
stems intact

2 tablespoons olive oil

1 teaspoon kosher salt

Freshly ground black pepper

1 cup crumbled feta (about 4 ounces)

1 cup pitted, roughly chopped Kalamata olives

1 English cucumber, cut into medium dice

1 cup grape tomatoes, halved

½ medium red onion, thinly sliced

Flaky sea salt

1. The Greek dressing does double duty as a marinade *and* a dressing. To make it, whisk the vinegar, garlic, honey, oregano, mustard, and salt and pepper to taste in a medium bowl. Slowly stream in the olive oil, whisking vigorously until emulsified. Adjust the seasoning if necessary.

2. Place the chicken in a zip-top bag with ½ cup of the dressing and marinate for 2 hours in the fridge. Cover the remaining dressing and set aside in the fridge.

3. Set a grill to medium heat. Oil the grates with the vegetable oil and grill the chicken breasts for 7 to 8 minutes on each side, until golden and the internal temperature is 165°F. Let rest for 5 to 10 minutes, then cut into ½-inch slices.

4. Turn the grill to high heat. Brush each half of the romaine hearts with the olive oil and grill on the cut sides until slightly charred, 2 to 3 minutes. Season the chicken with the kosher salt and ¼ teaspoon pepper.

5. Arrange the romaine on a serving platter. Sprinkle the chicken, feta, olives, cucumber, tomatoes, and onion directly on the romaine and drizzle with the reserved dressing. Top with a sprinkle of flaky sea salt and a few good grindings of pepper and get your summer on!

Crispy Mediterranean Chickpeas

MAKES ABOUT 3 CUPS

A chickpea is neither poultry nor a pea. Discuss . . . Oh, and if you can contain yourself and not eat all these in their first five minutes out of the oven, they go great on a salad or soup for a healthier protein-packed crouton.

Two 15-ounce cans chickpeas, drained, rinsed, and dried thoroughly so they are *super-duper dry*

¼ cup olive oil

2 teaspoons za'atar seasoning

1 teaspoon kosher salt

1. Preheat the oven to 400°F.

2. Toss the chickpeas with the oil, za'atar, and salt in a large bowl. Spread them on a rimmed sheet pan in an even layer. Bake until golden brown, 30 to 40 minutes, giving the pan a gentle but solid shake a couple of times as you bake.

3. Place the chickpeas on a paper towel–lined plate to absorb any excess oil. Store in an airtight container in the pantry for up to 1 week. These can get a little soft as they sit, so it's best to reheat them quickly in a 400°F oven for 5 minutes to refresh that crunch.

Crispy Skin Salmon

MAKES 4 SERVINGS

Sarah and I eat this at least once a week. I swear it keeps my hairline in check and my skin taut and bright. What I love about salmon is that one can only eat so much in one sitting. When cooked right (like in this recipe), it's so rich and buttery that you can't possibly eat more than a fillet and a half. It's just too good, too gratifying, too filling.

I tried to eat two fillets once, in the late aughts when I was pushing record-level pounds and had just discovered the power of well-prepared salmon. Being a typical amateur salmon eater, I went in for a second portion during a light luncheon and plowed right through it without even thinking about it. Needless to say, I didn't eat for the next day and half. Two days later, I noticed in the mirror while brushing my teeth that my hair was so long and lustrous it was dragging behind me on the bathroom floor, not unlike the train of a Bengali wedding gown. In fact, that afternoon while on my daily stroll through the local prairie, I was mistaken for a wild golden pony and rustled up by a band of unkempt yet kind horse thieves. After several intense hours of confusion, I eventually talked my way out of this pickle and made it back home safely, where I promptly booked a cut and color with my hair stylist, Michael, to make my hair less distractingly beautiful. It was one hell of a ride and quite frankly worth that extra portion. Just keep in mind that salmon is deceptively filling and oh so good for your skin and hair.

FISH TIP: *Salmon is best when the internal temperature hits 130°F to 135°F. Treat it just like a steak or burger and take its temp to keep it moist and flaky!*

1 tablespoon olive oil
Four 3- to 4-ounce skin-on Atlantic salmon
    fillets
1 teaspoon kosher salt
½ teaspoon freshly ground black pepper
2 tablespoons unsalted butter
2 garlic cloves, smashed
3 fresh thyme sprigs
Mashed Creamy Sweet Potatoes (recipe
    follows on page 135), for serving

1. Heat the oil in a 12-inch nonstick skillet over medium heat.
2. Pat the salmon fillets with paper towels to remove any excess moisture. Season with salt and pepper all over. Lay in the pan, skin side down, and sear for 7 to 8 minutes, until the skin is very crispy. Gently flip with a fish spatula and add the butter, garlic, and thyme.
3. Cook for 5 to 6 minutes, until the salmon reaches the desired temperature (see Fish Tip).
4. Serve immediately, skin side up, over the sweet potatoes with a spoon of the melted butter from the pan.

Put your ear up
to this page . . .
Can you hear the
ocean?

Mashed Creamy Sweet Potatoes

We are always flush with sweet potatoes here in the Mauro house. Sarah is obsessed and must consume at least one sweet potato a day. If she doesn't, she starts shaking, sweating, and hallucinating.

This is a quick and slightly indulgent method to help keep your sweet potato game fresh and exciting. It's also the perfect mattress for your Crispy Skin Salmon (page 133) to lay on—luxuriously soft yet firm enough not to cause lower-back issues or aggravate your sciatica.

¼ cup heavy (whipping) cream
3 tablespoons unsalted butter
3 medium sweet potatoes, peeled, quartered, and cut into ¼-inch wedges
2 tablespoons pure maple syrup
Kosher salt and freshly ground black pepper

1. Heat the cream and butter in a medium saucepan over low heat until the butter has melted.

2. Add the sweet potatoes. Gently simmer over low heat, covered and stirring frequently, for about 30 minutes, or until the potatoes are super tender. Add the maple syrup and mash with a potato masher until smooth and uniform. Season to taste with plenty of salt and pepper.

Greek Lemon Chicken and Orzo Bake

MAKES 4 SERVINGS

This is the easiest-to-execute recipe I have ever created. A true dump-and-stir dish and the only quintessential casserole in the book. Even though I don't call it a casserole in the title, let's be real: It's a casserole. Gus would not allow casseroles in the Mauro house. Pam would try a new casserole recipe recommended by one of her many friends (Barb, Linda, Linda, or the other Barb). Of course, they were always well executed, but Gus was never having it. And the guy eats *everything*. Even the discarded steak fat right off one of our plates. We once witnessed Gus eat a linen napkin with some spilled mint chocolate on it.

So, in honor of Gus, this dish is a *bake* and most certainly not a casserole.

Nonstick cooking spray
4 cups (1 quart) chicken stock
4 teaspoons kosher salt
2 teaspoons cornstarch
1 garlic clove, minced
Zest and juice of 2 lemons
2 fresh dill sprigs, minced, with a few small
    fronds reserved for garnish
1 cup orzo
1 teaspoon ground coriander
1 teaspoon freshly ground black pepper
Four 6-ounce boneless, skinless chicken breast
    halves, patted dry
2 lemons, cut into ¼-inch-thick slices

1. Preheat the oven to 375°F. Lightly grease a 9 × 13 glass baking dish with nonstick cooking spray.

2. Mix together the stock, 2 teaspoons of the salt, the cornstarch, garlic, lemon zest and juice, and minced dill in a large bowl. Add the orzo and mix until combined.

3. Mix together the coriander, pepper, and remaining 2 teaspoons salt in a small bowl. Coat the chicken breasts all over with the seasoning. This is not a place to have light fingers. Get every inch of the chicken coated.

4. Pour the orzo mixture into the prepared baking dish. Lay the chicken evenly on top and press down so that all but the tops of the breasts are submerged. Shingle half the lemon slices between the chicken breasts (reserve the rest for serving).

5. Bake, uncovered, for 40 minutes, until the chicken registers an internal temperature of 165°F. Let rest for 5 minutes. Top with some dainty dill fronds and serve with the reserved lemon slices. Store any leftovers in an airtight container in the fridge for up to 2 days.

This bake is quickly
approaching legend
status.

Imagine running into
these three thugs in
a dark alley.

The Juiciest Turkey Burgers Ever

MAKES 4 *GIANT* SANDWICHES

This tastes like a real turkey burger, not a turkey burger attempting to masquerade as a beef burger. The added richness from the ricotta ensures that each bite is juicy, and the sage and soy give it a festive umami angle that makes this burger its own flavor star.

TURKEY TIP: *Please take the internal temperature of this turkey while you cook. Please. And do not take it past 165°F. If one patty hits 165°F on an instant-read thermometer and the others are behind, take that one off! If you overcook these, you will know. If you cook them to 165°F, you will develop a recurring dream about them.*

2 pounds ground turkey (a bit of dark meat is preferred for flavor and fat)

¾ cup whole milk ricotta

2 tablespoons minced fresh sage

3 tablespoons soy sauce

2 teaspoons Worcestershire sauce

1 tablespoon Dijon mustard, plus more for the buns

1 teaspoon kosher salt

½ teaspoon freshly ground black pepper

1 tablespoon vegetable oil

4 tablespoons (½ stick) salted butter, at room temperature, for griddling

4 whole wheat buns

2 heirloom tomatoes, sliced ¼ inch thick (choose tomatoes large enough so that the slices will be bun-size)

Pickled red onions (see Note)

1. Combine the turkey, ricotta, sage, soy sauce, Worcestershire, mustard, salt, and pepper in a large bowl. Divide into 4 equal patties.

2. Heat the oil in a cast-iron skillet over medium-high heat. Add the patties, cover the pan, and sear until golden brown, 3 to 4 minutes. Flip, cover again, and cook for 3 to 4 minutes, until the internal temperature of each burger reaches 165°F. Remove from the heat and tent with foil to rest for at least 3 minutes.

3. As always, butter and griddle your bread! Set a large nonstick skillet over medium heat (you can use the skillet you just cooked the burgers in, but you should wipe it clean with a paper towel). Schmear butter on the inside sides of each bun and, working in batches, place butter side down on the skillet. Gently griddle until golden brown, about 5 minutes.

4. On the bottom bun, place a slice of heirloom tomato, then the turkey burger, then some pickled onions. Spread a nice crust-to-crust schmear of mustard on the top bun. Close and cut to admire the colorful and *inspiring* cross section. Take a bite and quickly forget about cows in general.

NOTE: *To make pickled red onions, simmer 1 cup red wine vinegar, ½ cup water, 2 tablespoons sugar, and 2 tablespoons kosher salt until dissolved. Cut 1 medium red onion into ¼-inch slices, add it to the pickling liquid, and let sit in the refrigerator overnight.*

Radiculous Radicchio Citrus Salad

MAKES 4 SERVINGS

Simple and colorful, this salad will brighten up any spread that needs a little sunshine.

2 navel oranges, zested and supremed (see below), juice reserved

2 tablespoons apple cider vinegar

1 tablespoon Dijon mustard

1 small shallot, minced (about 1 tablespoon)

½ cup extra virgin olive oil

Kosher salt and freshly ground black pepper

2 radicchio heads, torn into 1-inch pieces

2 bunches of watercress, washed, dried, and torn into bite-size pieces

1. Whisk the zest, reserved orange juice, vinegar, mustard, and shallot in a medium bowl. While whisking, slowly drizzle in the oil. Season to taste with salt and pepper.

2. Place the radicchio and watercress in a large bowl. Add the dressing to taste and toss. Top with the orange segments and serve. Take a bite and experience the cute interplay of sweet, bitter, tangy, and fruity. It's fun time, and you'll be glad you took this journey.

HOW TO SUPREME ORANGES (OR ANY CITRUS FRUIT)

1. Slice off a little of the top and bottom of the fruit to create a stable surface.

2. Using a sharp knife, trim away the skin and pith, following the natural curvature of the fruit. The goal is to expose the fruit while cutting away as little of it as possible.

3. Using a paring knife, cut out the segments of fruit. Do this over a bowl to catch any juice. Hold the fruit with a towel in your hand and for each segment, slice along both sides of the natural membrane until the segment drops into the bowl beneath.

4. Reserve the juice in the bowl for use in your vinaigrette!

The Post-Apocalyptic Smoothie

MAKES TWO 12-OUNCE SMOOTHIES

I tell Lorenzo this smoothie is the perfect post-apocalyptic source of sustenance. This combination of complex carbohydrates, easily digestible plant-based proteins, healthy fats, and vitamins contains everything the human system needs to give it the power to outrun fast-as-hell zombies and evade bands of malicious marauders looking to take your shit. It will supply you with enough energy to till fields so you can successfully farm your own food to help feed your progeny and begin the process of rebuilding a society from the ground up.

That being said, this is also perfect for a quick, *highly* nutritious non-apocalyptic breakfast that will sustain you and your loved ones for hours to come. It's great for post-workout recovery as well. And kids love it, too, guaranteed.

1 ripe banana
1 scoop vanilla protein powder
2 tablespoons peanut butter powder, such as PB2
¼ cup frozen spinach (just scoop right from the freezer bag)
1 teaspoon flax seeds
1 Medjool date, pitted
¼ cup fresh or frozen blueberries
1 cup ice cubes
1 to 1¼ cups unsweetened almond milk or other low-fat milk of your choice
Granola, for serving (I love the granola from ingrained Chicago)

Place everything in a blender and start zipping away. Add more milk if it's too thick, until your desired consistency is achieved. Pour into glasses and top with granola. Suck this baby down with a big ol' environmentally friendly straw and quickly feel the *power* and accept the newfound motivation and stamina to *finally achieve your dreams.*

Emily, me, and Gus with
cousins Katy and D'Maglio
in the back!

7

WE'RE THROWING A PROPER FIESTA

I've traveled to Mexico more than any other destination or country. From Ensenada to Valle de Guadalupe, from Tulum to Xpu Há, and from Puerto Vallarta to Ixtapa, I've fallen deeply in love with the Mexican culture, people, and food. These are my favorites not only to make and serve but also to eat.

Roasted Mexican Street Corn Salad

MAKES 6 TO 8 SERVINGS

I love the flavor and summer vibe of true street cart Mexican elotes: whole ears of corn smothered in mayo, cotija cheese, cilantro, and spices. What I don't love is the mess, the overabundance of hot mayo, and, quite frankly, the mess of an overabundance of hot mayo.

This is all those phenomenal flavors but in a prettier and more portable package that is perfect for any BBQ spread, holiday table, or family fiesta.

EL CONSEJO: *There are two schools of thought when it comes to creamy side salads: You either serve them immediately or let them ripen in the fridge overnight. Unlike slaws and potato salad, this salad is best and brightest when mixed fresh and served immediately.*

Vegetable oil, for greasing

6 ears of corn, husked

4 green onions

1 red bell pepper

2 jalapeños

¼ cup mayonnaise

⅓ cup sour cream

Zest and juice of 1 lime

1 garlic clove, grated on a Microplane

1 teaspoon chipotle powder

1 teaspoon hot sauce

One 15-ounce can black beans, drained and rinsed

Kosher salt and freshly ground black pepper

¼ cup chopped fresh cilantro

8 bacon slices, cooked using the Mauro Method (see page 19), roughly chopped

continues

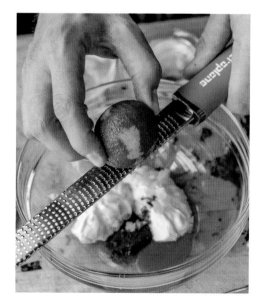

1. Set a grill to high and oil the grates well with vegetable oil.

2. Place the corn, green onions, red bell pepper, and jalapeños directly on the grates. Grill until charred on all sides. The corn will take 8 to 10 minutes, the onions about 12 minutes, the bell pepper about 15 minutes, and the jalapeños 8 to 10 minutes. Set aside to cool.

3. Whisk the mayo, sour cream, lime zest and juice, garlic, chipotle powder, and hot sauce in a medium bowl. Set aside.

4. Slice the corn kernels from the cobs. Remove the ribs and seeds from the red pepper and cut it into medium dice. Core, seed, and mince the jalapeños. Thinly slice the white parts of the green onions.

5. Place the corn, bell pepper, green onions, black beans, and jalapeños in a large bowl. Mix in half the dressing while the veggies are still slightly warm. Season with salt and pepper to taste and add more dressing if desired. Store any remaining dressing in an airtight container in the fridge for up to 2 weeks.

6. Top with the fresh cilantro and crispy bacon and serve immediately.

Pickled Jalapeños with Carrots and Onions

MAKES 1 QUART

These are a perfect and way more flavorful version of the Mexican table staple you are automatically served alongside your chips and salsa. I usually start with a couple of carrots, maybe a slice of onion, and then work up the courage to take a bite out of one of the whole jalapeños. Yes, that bite is usually very spicy, but it's the accompanying flavors that make that spice totally addictive.

2 tablespoons vegetable oil

4 garlic cloves

2 medium carrots, cut on the bias into ½-inch-thick slices

12 large jalapeños, cut into ½-inch-thick slices

½ medium white onion, cut into ⅛-inch-thick slices

½ cup apple cider vinegar

2 bay leaves

½ teaspoon dried thyme

½ teaspoon Mexican oregano

4 black peppercorns

½ teaspoon kosher salt

1. Heat the oil in a medium skillet over medium heat. Add the garlic and fry for about 3 minutes, until lightly browned. Remove from the oil and set aside.

2. Add the carrots, jalapeños, and onion to the same skillet and fry, stirring frequently, for about 5 minutes, until the veggies soften a little.

3. Add ½ cup water, the browned garlic, vinegar, bay leaves, thyme, oregano, peppercorns, and salt. Cover, bring to a simmer, and cook for 9 to 10 minutes, until the carrots start to soften. Remove from the heat and place in a quart-size mason jar or other heatproof container. Let cool, then place in the fridge overnight to let all those flavors mingle. Store in an airtight container in the refrigerator for up to 1 month.

The perfect summer salad

Grilled Pineapple Guacamole

MAKES 4 TO 6 SERVINGS

I know, I know . . . some say adding fruit to guacamole is sacrilege. Guess what? I break rules. I live life on the edge. I don't abide by what *the man* dictates. They call me the James Dean of food, and I swear I am dangerously close to getting a forehead tattoo that reads "naughty boy." Don't mess with me or try to box me in. Capisce?

The charred pineapple in this recipe adds a sweet blast of fruity acidity and smoky flavor that helps amplify the entire bowl of guac to a very addictive chip-dippable eating experience.

TIP/TYP/TIHP: *Do not neglect smooshing only two of the avocados and leaving one to dice up. The texture variation is a guaranteed mouth pleaser.*

Vegetable oil, for greasing
½ fresh pineapple, peeled and cut into 2 thick rings, or 2 precut store-bought rings
3 ripe avocados
Juice of 2 limes
¼ teaspoon ground cumin
½ teaspoon kosher salt, plus more as needed
¼ teaspoon freshly ground black pepper, plus more as needed
¼ cup minced fresh cilantro
1 Fresno chile, diced (cored and seeded if you want less heat)
1 teaspoon Tajín seasoning (optional)
Tortilla chips, for serving

1. Oil a grill or grill pan and preheat to high heat.

2. Grill the pineapple on both sides until charred. Let cool completely, remove the core if you haven't already, and cut into ¼-inch pieces. Set aside.

3. Scoop the flesh from 2 of the avocados into a large bowl. Mash and season with the lime juice, cumin, salt, and pepper. Dice the remaining avocado and gently fold it into the mashed avocado. Stir in the cilantro and half the Fresno chile.

4. Now it's time to taste the guac to check for heat and salt levels. Add more salt and pepper if needed. Top with the charred pineapple. Add the Tajín on top and more of the Fresno chile if you're feeling feisty.

5. Serve with chips and a big ol' smile!

Fire this up on a blustery
autumnal evening.

Black Bean and Roasted Tomato Soup with Avocado Crema

MAKES 4 SERVINGS

I 100 percent credit this recipe to my very loyal and talented recipe tester, Lisa Krych. She is actually more than just a recipe tester; she's also a gifted food stylist and recipe developer and an amazing chef. This soup is all her, and it's frickin' wonderful. It's a great spin on traditional black bean soup.

½ pound smoked bacon or pancetta, cut into ½-inch pieces

1 medium yellow onion, minced

2 garlic cloves, minced

One 14.5-ounce can fire-roasted diced tomatoes

1 cup chicken stock

2 chipotle chiles in adobo, chopped fine

Three 15-ounce cans black beans, including canning liquid

1 bay leaf

1 teaspoon kosher salt

1 jalapeño, cored, seeded, and sliced thin, for garnish

1 small bunch of cilantro, for garnish

AVOCADO CREMA

½ cup Mexican crema or sour cream

2 ripe avocados, pitted, peeled, and roughly chopped

Zest and juice of 2 to 3 limes, as needed

Kosher salt and freshly ground black pepper

1. Set a medium saucepan or Dutch oven over medium-high heat. Add the bacon and cook until crispy, 5 to 6 minutes. Transfer to a paper towel–lined plate, leaving the fat in the pan.

2. Quickly add the onion and cook it in the bacon grease, stirring occasionally, for 5 minutes, letting it get some good color. Add the garlic and cook for 1 minute, until fragrant.

3. Add the tomatoes, stock, chiles, beans, bay leaf, and salt. Bring to a boil, then reduce the heat, cover, and simmer for at least 30 minutes, until the beans are tender, stirring occasionally.

4. To make the avocado crema, place the crema, avocados, and lime zest and juice of 2 of the limes in the bowl of a food processor and blend until smooth. If too thick, thin out with a bit more lime juice. Season to taste with salt and pepper.

5. Transfer the avocado crema to a bowl and cover the surface with plastic wrap to keep it from browning. Refrigerate the bowl.

6. Now back to the soup. Carefully remove the bay leaf and discard. Using an immersion blender, blend the soup until you achieve the constancy you desire; I like mine thick and chunky. (If you do not have an immersion blender, transfer the soup to a regular blender, but remove the plastic piece in the lid, place a kitchen towel over the top, and start on low. This will keep pressure from building up and causing the lid to pop off.) Taste and season with more salt if desired.

7. When ready to serve, retrieve your avocado crema chillin' in the fridge. Ladle the soup into bowls and garnish with the bacon, avocado crema, jalapeños, and cilantro. Store leftovers in an airtight container in the fridge for up to 3 days, or in the freezer for up to 3 months.

Whole Mojo Chicken

MAKES 4 TO 6 SERVINGS

This dish is all about that zesty Cuban-inspired mojo marinade. It turns a humble whole chicken into a *fiesta cubana* on your tongue. Your taste buds will be swooned into submission by the Afro-beat rhythm of the timbales, blaring trumpets, and jazzy minor seventh chords tinkling from the piano.

BEST. TIP. EVER: *This goes great with a fresh mojito while you wear a brimmed fedora and a breathable hand-stitched guayabera.*

Zest of 1 orange (about 1 tablespoon)
Juice of 2 oranges (about ½ cup)
Juice of 2 limes (about 4 tablespoons)
4 garlic cloves, roughly chopped
1 small yellow onion, finely chopped
1 tablespoon chili powder
1 tablespoon ground cumin
1 tablespoon kosher salt
1 tablespoon canola oil
One 4-pound chicken, patted dry (I like air chilled)
Vegetable oil, for greasing

1. To make the mojo marinade, whisk the orange zest, orange juice, lime juice, garlic, onion, chili powder, cumin, salt, and canola oil in a medium bowl.

2. Reserve half the marinade for basting. Transfer the other half to a large zip-top bag and add the chicken. Seal the bag and squish the marinade around to ensure the chicken gets coated. Marinate the chicken in the refrigerator for at least 4 hours or up to 6 hours.

3. Set up a grill for indirect cooking (one hot side, one cool side), with an ideal temp hovering around 300°F, and oil the grates with the vegetable oil. Place the chicken on the cool side of the grill (right side up) and get to cooking. Every 15 minutes, baste the bird with the reserved marinade, then carefully rotate the bird 180 degrees. Cook until the thickest part of the breast reaches 160°F and thickest part of the thigh registers 165°F, 60 to 75 minutes, depending on how you control your heat.

4. Adjust an oven rack to the lower position and preheat the oven to broil.

5. Place the chicken on a sheet pan and broil in the oven until the skin is extra crispy, 2 to 3 minutes. You can definitely do this on the hot side of the grill, but I find that with whole birds, the skin tends to rip and tear easily. If you use the broiler, there is a lot less futzing with the bird and you keep that delectable skin intact!

6. Let the chicken rest for at least 10 minutes and the carry-over cooking will take the internal temperature to the perfect 165°F for the breast and 170°F for the thigh. Carve and serve. Leftovers can be stored in an airtight container in the fridge for up to 2 days.

¡Dude!

Slice against
the grain!

The Perfect Charred Carne Asada

MAKES 4 TO 6 SERVINGS

When a Mexican joint does carne asada very well, chances are the rest of the offerings will follow suit. It's the benchmark for a great Mexican dining experience. What I look for is a pronounced well-seasoned char with a juicy medium interior.

The key to a great asada is using outside skirt steak—by far the most underrated cut of meat. The outside skirt is far more flavorful, marbled, and tender than the inside cut. Unfortunately, the inside skirt is the more common cut in grocery stores, so seek out outside skirts through your butcher or grocery store meat guy. Or you can order them online delivered to your door through Mauro Provisions (mauroprovisions.com), my online butcher shop!

MAXIMUM TIPIUM: *Make sure you dry the steak out with salt overnight. It's a fast pass to maximum char.*

1½ pounds outside skirt steak (about 2 long steaks)
Vegetable oil, for greasing
1 teaspoon kosher salt
½ teaspoon freshly ground black pepper
4 to 5 red jalapeños
12 warm small corn tortillas, for serving
Rajas (page 159), for serving
2 or 3 limes, sliced into wedges, for serving
1 small bunch of cilantro, roughly chopped, for serving

continues

Dry it out!

Sear it up!

1. Remove the steaks from the butcher paper and pat them dry with a paper towel. Place them on a wire rack in a rimmed sheet pan and refrigerate, uncovered, for at least 2 hours. This will ensure the steaks get a beautiful rich color when grilled.

2. Preheat the grill to medium-high, making sure those grates are nice and hot. Oil the grates with the vegetable oil. (If you have a side burner to your grill, this is a great time to use it to make the rajas.)

3. Give the steaks a generous sprinkle of salt and pepper, then place them on the hottest section of the grill. Grill for 3 to 5 minutes, until nicely charred, then flip and grill for 3 to 5 minutes more, until the meat registers 140°F with an instant-read thermometer. Place the jalapeños on the grill and allow them to char, 3 to 4 minutes per side. I love serving these whole alongside the steak. Very traditional and very adventurous for those who want to go in for a quick bite with each bite of steak!

4. Remove the steaks and set them on a cutting board. Slice the steaks in half with the grain. Now turn them 90 degrees and slice against the grain into ¼-inch strips. Those little end pieces? Just pop those right in ya mouth. I call those chef snacks!

5. Make a big platter with the tortillas, rajas, charred jalapeños, limes, and cilantro and call in the troops!

Rajas

MAKES ABOUT 2 CUPS

This traditional and simple recipe was developed by my culinary partner and left-hand lady, Lisa Krych. You see, Lisa knows a ton about Mexican cuisine as she worked for legendary chef Rick Bayless for many years. When I gave her my original rajas recipe, she immediately threw it away and said I was overcomplicating things. I did not resist. I listened, learned, and realized that the key is the Mexican oregano, which has tight little buds that just explode with floral flavor.

Rajas go great on tacos and nachos, on top of salads, or just eaten plain out of a bowl if you're feeling a bit sluggish.

4 medium poblano chiles
2 tablespoons vegetable oil
1 large yellow onion, cut into ¼-inch slices
½ teaspoon dried Mexican oregano
2 garlic cloves, minced
Kosher salt and freshly ground black pepper

1. Roast the poblanos directly on the grates of your gas burner set to medium. Turn every couple of minutes to char them evenly on all sides, about 10 minutes total. If you don't have gas burners, then use a very hot grill or place the poblanos on a medium sheet pan on the top rack in the oven and broil for 10 minutes or until charred, turning frequently to char all sides. Place the charred chiles in a bowl, cover with a kitchen towel, and let rest for about

5 minutes. Now you'll be able to rub off the blackened skin with ease. Remove the stems and seedpods and gently wipe away the charred skin with a paper towel. Cut into ¼-inch strips and set aside.

2. Heat the vegetable oil in a 12-inch skillet over medium-high heat, add the onion, and sauté for 6 to 7 minutes. You want the onion to brown but still be crunchy. Add the poblanos, garlic, and oregano. Stir until the garlic is fragrant, about 1 minute, season to taste with salt and pepper, and serve immediately or store in the fridge in an airtight container for up to 2 days.

Charred Table Salsa

MAKES ABOUT 3 CUPS

There's nothing like fresh homemade salsa, and there's nothing better than this version. It goes splendidly with any chip, any fish, and any meat. It's truly the last salsa recipe you'll ever need.

EL JEFFERINO'S SALSA TIP: *Serve this at room temp. Right-from-the-fridge salsa tends to have muted flavors.*

3 large tomatillos (about ¾ pound), husks removed, cleaned
1 small yellow onion, sliced into ½-inch rings
2 Roma tomatoes
1 poblano chile
3 garlic cloves, skin on
1 dried ancho chile, seeded and cut in half
Juice of 1 lime
¼ cup fresh cilantro leaves
1 teaspoon agave
Kosher salt and freshly ground black pepper

1. Adjust an oven rack to the highest position and preheat the oven to broil.

2. Arrange the tomatillos, onion, tomatoes, poblano, and garlic on an unlined rimmed sheet pan. Broil for about 5 minutes, until the skin of the tomatillos blisters and blackens. Remove the garlic and flip everything else to the other side. Broil for another 5 minutes to blacken. Set aside to cool.

3. Place the ancho chile in a small dry skillet over high heat. Meanwhile, get some water boiling (I always use my teakettle!). Using a metal spatula, press down on the chile for a few seconds, until it starts to change color. Flip over and repeat. Place the charred chile in a small bowl and add boiling water to cover completely. Let sit until the chile is softened, 8 to 10 minutes. Reserve the water to adjust the consistency of your salsa, if needed.

4. Skin, core, and seed the charred poblano. Free the garlic cloves from their skins. Leave the charred skin on the tomatillos. Place the poblano, garlic, tomatillos, and onion (including any juices left behind) in the bowl of a food processor.

5. Fish out the steeped ancho chile and add it, along with the tomatoes, lime juice, cilantro, and agave to the food processor, and blend until mostly smooth. Adjust the consistency with the reserved chile water, if desired. Season to taste with salt and pepper.

Put a chip in me now.

Three tacos are never
enough, right?

Crispy Carnitas for a Crowd

MAKES 4 TO 6 SERVINGS

This is my most favorite pork dish on the planet. There are a bunch of more traditional and cumbersome ways to prepare true carnitas, but this method gives you all the succulence with a ton of ease.

One 4-pound pork shoulder, cut into 2-inch
    cubes, with the fat cap intact
Kosher salt and freshly ground black pepper
1 medium yellow onion, quartered
3 garlic cloves, smashed
Zest and juice of 1 large orange (about ¼ cup
    juice and 1 tablespoon zest), squished slices
    reserved
2 cinnamon sticks
1 cup vegetable oil
1 small bunch of fresh cilantro, for garnish
Corn tortillas, for serving
Grilled Pineapple Guacamole (page 150), for
    serving
Salsa Verde (page 164), for serving
Fresh lime slices, for serving

1. Preheat the oven to 275°F.
2. Place the pork chunks in a large disposable aluminum pan and season all over with salt and pepper. Place any chunks with a fat cap upright. Nestle in the onion, garlic, juiced orange slices, and cinnamon sticks. Sprinkle the orange zest over everything, then pour on the orange juice and oil. Cover tightly with foil and cook until very tender, 3 to 4 hours. (This step can be done a day ahead. Just keep the fat and rendered juices in the pan, cover tightly, and refrigerate.)
3. Carefully drain the liquid into a fat separator or measuring cup. Lightly pull the pork chunks apart with two forks until just shredded but not pulverized.
4. Set a large nonstick skillet over medium heat. Brush both sides of the tortillas with some of the pork fat that the carnitas are swimming in and griddle until bubbly, 2 to 3 minutes on each side. Set aside, wrapped in a towel or tortilla warmer.
5. Place the pork in a 12-inch nonstick skillet with ¼ to ½ cup of the reserved cooking liquid. Bring to a simmer and watch as the pork gets super crispy on the bottom and the fat and skin start to sizzle and fry. No need to turn or flip. When the bottom is golden and crispy, 8 to 10 minutes, remove from the heat and place the pork on a plate. I like to invert it from the pan onto the plate so the golden brown crispy side is facing up.
6. Garnish with cilantro and serve with the tortillas, guacamole, salsa verde, and lime slices.

Salsa Verde

There is a distinct difference between jarred salsas and homemade fresh salsas. There are many great jarred salsas out there that have the ability to complement any tortillas chip they come in contact with. However, nothing compares to that moment in making a fresh salsa from scratch when you first take the lid off the food processor and you're hit with a waft of aroma that simultaneously stings your eyeballs and makes your mouth salivate. That's the magic. Then you take a bite and never buy a jar of salsa again.

3 large tomatillos (about ¾ pound), husks removed, cleaned
1 small white onion, sliced into ½-inch rings
1 jalapeño
3 garlic cloves, skin on
Juice of 1 lime, plus more as desired
¼ cup fresh chopped cilantro leaves
Kosher salt

1. Adjust an oven rack to the highest position and preheat the broiler.

2. Arrange the tomatillos, onion, jalapeño, and garlic on an unlined rimmed sheet pan. Broil for about 5 minutes, until the skin of the tomatillos blisters and blackens. Remove the garlic and flip everything else to the other side. Broil for another 5 minutes to blacken. Set aside to cool.

3. When cool enough to handle, remove the stem from the charred jalapeño, and if you want to tame the majority of the heat, remove all the seeds and ribs. If you want this salsa *poppin'*, then remove *nothing*! Free the garlic cloves from their skins. Leave the charred skin on the tomatillos. Place the jalapeño, garlic, tomatillos, and onion (including any juices left behind) in the bowl of a food processor. Add the lime juice, cilantro, and salt to taste and blend until mostly smooth. Taste for seasoning and add more salt and lime juice if needed. Serve warm or at room temperature. Store in an airtight container for up to a week. If you have the foresight, let the salsa come to room temp before serving. The subtle warmth really reawakens the flavors.

Citrusy Honey-Tequila Shrimp

MAKES 4 SERVINGS

To flambé is to use the power of flammable booze to ignite your dish in a hot glow of orange fire. This adds a last-minute boozy char to your shrimp and should be done *off* the heat, away from the stovetop's flame and using a long stick lighter. This is not the time to get all mid-century baked Alaska and burn down your kitchen curtains.

Vegetable oil, for greasing
1 pound shrimp (16 to 20), peeled and
    deveined
2 tablespoons honey
2 tablespoons clementine, tangerine, or
    orange juice
Zest and juice of 1 lime
¼ teaspoon ground cumin
¼ teaspoon chipotle powder
½ teaspoon kosher salt, plus more to taste
1 tablespoon olive oil
Freshly ground black pepper
2 ounces blanco tequila or 2 ounces fresh
    orange juice with a dash of white vinegar
2 tablespoons finely chopped cilantro, for
    garnish

1. Preheat an indoor grill plate over high heat and oil the grate.

2. Mix together the honey, clementine juice, lime zest and juice, cumin, chipotle powder, and salt in a medium bowl. Add the shrimp, toss to coat, and marinate in the fridge for 15 minutes.

3. Set a strainer over a medium bowl and drain the shrimp completely, reserving the marinade. Pat the shrimp dry with paper towels, toss it with the oil, and season with salt and pepper.

4. Grill on high on both sides until super charred and no longer opaque in the middle, 2 to 3 minutes on each side.

5. Set a large skillet over medium-high heat. Add the reserved marinade, bring to a simmer, and cook until reduced by half, 3 to 5 minutes. Add the shrimp. Now it's time to deglaze with the tequila. Continue to simmer until the shrimp are nice and sticky and the sauce is thick enough to coat the back of a spoon. Garnish with chopped cilantro and serve immediately.

8

I KNOW I'M GOING TO REGRET SAYING THIS, BUT . . .
WE'RE HOSTING THE HOLIDAYS THIS YEAR

We literally start planning our Christmas Eve menu in June. It's a tremendous amount of work, as we host thirty-one people in our home. It's exhausting, exhilarating, and eventually, rewarding. There's always talk of catering or scaling back or keeping it simple, but we always end up going *all in* and overdoing it. So, swing for the fences. Put on your finest sweater, crank up the Frank Sinatra album *A Jolly Christmas*, and go to town.

« Gus, Pam, Sarah, Emily, me, Cousin Dan; in the background, Cousin Annie

Grandma Kay's Sausage Bread

MAKES 4 TO 6 SERVINGS

My grandmother Catherine Renzi was the best "cousins' grandma" anyone can ask for.

What do I mean by "cousins' grandma"? I have fourteen first cousins on my mother's side, and my grandma Kay was the coolest damn grandma a bunch of super-close cousins could ever wish for. We all lived within minutes of each other and would frequently convene for hangouts and sleepovers at Gram's house, a tiny black-and-white two-bedroom cottage on Neva in the Galewood neighborhood right on the edge of the Northwest Side of Chicago. When we were by Gram's house, it was never dull—partially due to the fact that it was always full of at least a dozen cousins.

Grandma Kay created a very free environment for us to let loose in, far from the judging glares of our parents. Those nights, Gram's house belonged to all of us from the

Mauro/Renzi/Berni/Speziale crew: Nick, Gina, Dan, Dave, Jessica, Chrissie, Jenny, Frank, Alison, Joe, Jeff, Emily, Danny, Melissa, and finally, the baby of the family, my sister Dana.

We would put on talent shows or plays. We would run around the neighborhood and play pool on the billiards table in the creepy and dank unfinished basement. Grandma Kay would brew us espresso with a ton of sugar while teaching us the ins and outs of proper poker. We each had our own recycled Parmesan containers filled with coins to gamble with. Real money won; real money lost. She taught us how to hold our cards "abreast," when to ante up, and when to "fold 'em."

Can you picture the wonderland of a dozen or so children chugging sugared-up caffeine while gambling into the wee early hours of Sunday morning? We'd all eventually crash wherever we could crash. Grandpa Joe and Gram would sleep in their bedroom; the other bedroom fit at least four kids in one bed. The frunchroom held only Grandpa Joe's chair and that old cliché of a plastic-covered sofa. The TV room in the back had a couch to crash on, too. Kids would end up everywhere. I usually took the frunchroom couch and would have to peel my skin off the plastic in the morning, much like a strawberry Fruit Roll-Up from its wrapper.

We'd always wake up at dawn at the sound of my Grandpa Joe, aka Pa, flipping pancakes and lighting his first Garcia y Vega cigar of the day. Gram slept much later. She was cool like that. Eventually she'd wake up and make us more sugary espresso. We would eat fried pizza

In my family,
this ruins dinners . . .

dough and pancakes while counting our coins, taking account of the previous night's poker winnings or losses. Gram would start cooking sauce and baking off sausage bread for Sunday dinner. The swirling scent of fragrant sauce, cigar smoke, and espresso quickly filled the tiny house—and then all our parents would arrive. The sleepover was officially over and all power relinquished back to our folks. We didn't care. We all had one hell of a night.

Although the sleepover was over, time with family wasn't. We all would dine together, somehow, in that very small house. The cousins crowded the kids' table in the kitchen, rehashing war stories from the sleepover, while the parents maxed out the dining room, nursing hangovers from their wild, kid-free nights while praying they weren't going to have to occupy Pa's hot seat, a notorious table position directly next to Pa reserved for a son-in-law on his shit list. Usually Gus.

Grandma Kay peacefully passed away in 2018, and up to the end she still brought her famous sausage bread to every single family get-together. Well, that is, up until she guest-starred in an episode of *Sandwich King*. We made sausage bread together in front of the cameras, and naturally, she hit it out of the park. She truly relished every moment. By the time she received full hair and makeup and was escorted to the set, she became the star, performer, and diva she always deserved to be. After the segment aired and everybody showered her performance in praise, she decided it was best to retire from sausage-bread making. "It's on the internet now," she claimed, "so why the hell do you need me?" So now we make it. My cousin Joe does a great rendition, as do I. Most of us Mauro/Renzi/Berni/Speziale cousins do our best to carry on the tradition. I know she would be tickled and proud. But nothing will ever compare to that tray of warm sausage bread served up by Gram, in Gram's house during that golden era of Sunday dinners, when we would all get together, no matter what, to eat, laugh, and argue. Rest in peace, Gram. Love you.

2 tablespoons olive oil, plus more for brushing
1 pound sweet Italian sausage links, casings removed
4 ounces Genoa salami, cut into thin strips
2 cups shredded whole milk mozzarella (about 8 ounces)
Vegetable oil cooking spray
Flour, for the work surface
1 recipe Detroit-Style Pizza Dough (page 203) or 1 pound store-bought (Grandma Kay used a 1-pound loaf of thawed Rhodes pizza dough and let it rise per the instructions)

The sausage Holy Trinity

1. Preheat the oven to 340°F. This is admittedly odd, but she claimed it was the perfect temperature. You gonna argue with Gram? Aim for a hair under 350°F.

2. Heat the olive oil in a medium sauté pan over medium-high heat, add the sausages, and cook until brown, 12 to 15 minutes, breaking them up as they cook. Let cool.

3. Using a slotted spoon, transfer the sausage to a medium bowl and add the salami and mozzarella. Mix with your hands.

4. Spray a half-sheet pan with cooking spray.

5. On a floured surface, roll out the dough into one long 18 × 6-inch oval. Brush the dough with olive oil and sprinkle the sausage mixture all over, leaving a 1-inch perimeter uncovered. Gently stretch one long side of the dough and fold it so that it covers half the mixture. Tuck in the short ends to trap all that meat inside and roll it onto itself so the seam of the dough is on the bottom. We are looking for two revolutions. Shape the log into a slight crescent. Gently transfer to the prepared sheet pan. Poke holes along the top with a fork to release the steam while cooking.

6. Bake until very light brown on top, about 20 minutes.

7. Let rest for 10 minutes, then slice into 1-inch medallions. Plate and serve at any and all parties you host or attend for the rest of your natural-born life. You can make it a day ahead, wrap in foil and plastic wrap, and store in the fridge. Just reheat for 15 minutes in a 350°F oven. If you need to make it more than a day ahead, wrap in foil, *then* plastic wrap, and freeze for up to 2 months. Thaw completely at room temperature for 3 hours, remove the plastic wrap, and bake in *just foil* in a 350°F oven for 15 minutes. Leftovers should be wrapped in foil and stored in the fridge for up to 3 days. Just reheat wrapped in foil for 10 minutes in a 350°F oven.

Pre-roll

I know . . . I know . . .
get your head out of the gutter

Easy Porchetta

Porchetta is one of those dishes that when all the notes hit, the eating experience is an ethereal barrage on the senses, with pops of crispy pork skin, succulent unctuous meat dripping down your gullet, soft garlic, floral herbs, juicy loin, and loads of buttery fat. Problem is, making it perfect is really hard to do and takes a ton of technique and kitchen space.

I came up with this recipe as a way to deliver all the wonderment I waxed poetic about above—without all the damn work. By using a whole pork shoulder, you get it all: crispy fat cap and soft, well-rendered meat—and fat for days. It's much easier and just as delicious.

Don't be skeeved out by the anchovies. They give it a blast of funky salt that a true porchetta always brings to the party.

2 to 4 canned or jarred anchovies

¼ cup extra virgin olive oil

6 garlic cloves

¼ cup fresh oregano leaves

¼ cup fresh flat-leaf parsley leaves, more for garnish

2 tablespoons chopped fresh sage

2 tablespoons fresh thyme leaves

Zest and juice of 1 lemon

1 tablespoon kosher salt, plus more to taste

1 teaspoon freshly ground black pepper, plus more to taste

One 4- to 5-pound boneless pork shoulder, fat cap intact

Lemon wedges, for serving

1. To make the rub, combine the anchovies, oil, garlic, oregano, parsley, sage, thyme, lemon zest and juice, salt, and pepper in a food processor and buzz into a puree.

2. Adjust an oven rack to the lower position and preheat the oven to 275°F.

3. Butterfly your pork. Place the meat skin / fat cap side down on your cutting board. Using a sharp knife, slice the pork parallel to the counter about 2 inches from the bottom. Slice through, stopping ½ inch before the edge, then open the meat to lie flat like a book.

4. Rub half the herb-anchovy mixture all over the inside of the pork. Roll it up and, using butcher's twine, tie it very tightly about every 2 inches. Score any visible fat in a crosshatch pattern and season the outside with the remaining herb-anchovy mixture and more salt and pepper. Place the pork on a roasting rack in a roasting pan, fat cap side facing up, and pour 1 cup water in the bottom of the pan to keep the drippings from burning.

5. Roast until super fork tender and "pullable" and the internal temp registers 200°F, about 3½ to 4½ hours. Remove from the oven and let rest for at least 20 minutes.

6. Pour the liquid and renderings from the roasting pan into a small saucepan and simmer over medium heat until slightly reduced, 10 to 15 minutes. Season to taste.

7. Either pull or carve the roast. I like to carve it so you can see the stuffed interior. Place on a platter, garnish with plenty of parsley, and serve with the pan sauce and lemon wedges. Leftovers can be stored in an airtight container in the fridge for up to 3 days.

Madone!

Perfect
doneness!

Classic Beef Tenderloin

MAKES 6 TO 8 SERVINGS

Lorenzo and I are part of a father–son institution called the Indian Guides (hello to my fellow Kickapoo Tribe). A bunch of fathers and their young sons go camping every season, rain, snow, ice, or shine, and earn badges together shooting .22s, making fires, and competing against other groups in fairly intense canoe races. I'm going to be honest: The conditions are not ideal or comfortable. The weather is often horrendous, and there is little to zero sleep. That being said, it's 100 percent worth it for the quality one-on-one father–son time you get to spend with your boy—and for the legendary campfire meal.

While other tribes are burning hot dogs on muddy sticks, the mighty members of the Kickapoo Tribe have imported and prepared a smorgasbord of fine foodstuffs, like homemade Bolognese with fresh rigatoni, Caprese salads, and prime tenderloins, basted in butter and served with a rich mushroom sauce and creamy horseradish. I'm always on tenderloin duty. It's my charge and honor, and I will always put forth all the effort necessary to make it perfect using minimal cookware and resources. If they offered a tenderloin badge, my Indian Guides vest would be covered in them.

That's why this main-event steak dish is perfect for any get-together. It's easy to prep (if I can make it at a campsite, you can make it anywhere!), easy to make ahead if necessary, simple to serve, and, most important, buttery, supple, and beefy.

CHEFFREY'S CHEF NOTE: *The beauty of this reverse-sear method is that the meat does not need to rest, since it basically already rested in the oven. Also, you can make this an hour or two ahead of time and pan-sear and butter-baste right before serving.*

One 3- to 4-pound center-cut beef tenderloin, trimmed
1 to 2 teaspoons coarse sea salt
1 teaspoon freshly ground black pepper
2 tablespoons olive oil
2 tablespoons unsalted butter
1 recipe Honey-Horseradish Crema (page 179), for serving
1 recipe Mushroom and Red Wine Steak Sauce (page 180), for serving

1. Using kitchen twine, tie the roast every 2 inches, firmly but not *too* tight; it still needs to "breathe." Let the beef stand at room temperature for 1 hour before roasting.

2. Adjust an oven rack to the middle position and preheat the oven to 400°F.

3. Set the beef on a sheet pan fitted with a wire rack and season it all over with the salt and pepper.

4. Roast until the temperature of the center of the roast registers 125°F for medium-rare, about 40 to 55 minutes, or 135°F for medium, about 55 to 70 minutes. Anything longer than that and we shouldn't be friends.

5. Set a large cast-iron skillet over high heat. Add the oil, then the tenderloin, and sear for

continues

about 2 minutes on one side. Add the butter and turn the tenderloin a quarter turn. Sear each quadrant for 2 minutes. While cooking, constantly tilt the pan and, using a large spoon, scoop up the hot butter and baste the exposed tenderloin. When the entire tenderloin is browned, remove from the heat.

6. Remove the twine and cut the tenderloin into beautiful ½-inch-thick medallions. Serve immediately, spooning some of that hot basting butter all over the top.

7. Serve with the crema and steak sauce. Yes, two sauces. Give people the option, or drizzle on both of them and live like you're in the wilderness with your son and you might get eaten by a bear tomorrow anyway. Leftovers can be stored in an airtight container in the fridge for up to 2 days, or use them for my fantastic Chicago Cheesesteak (page 232).

AT THE CAMPSITE, the only cookware available is a horrendous ancient charcoal mini grill. Therefore, I come prepared with a giant stainless-steel skillet and butane turkey-fryer burner. Picture me, kneeling in the dank mud, in cold wind and whipping rain, headlamp illuminating the pan a mere 12 inches from the ground, while I sear and aggressively butter-baste this huge prime tenderloin before I pull out not my pocketknife but my trusty instant-read digital thermometer and probe the tenderloin, watching it hit a perfect 125°F. Never give up.

Honey-Horseradish Crema

MAKES ABOUT 1 CUP

The most underrated flavor is *nose heat*—that upper-sinus burn you get when you dunk your egg roll into too big of a puddle of Chinese hot mustard or schmear on way too much wasabi on that crispy dynamite dragon-breath rainbow roll. It comes on like a straight right jab to the septum, but luckily it subsides quickly, until all that's left is the pleasure that is the absence of pain—and an overwhelming urge to do it all over again.

If I'm dunking tender, well-marbled beef into creamy horseradish sauce, I want it to, in the words of John Cougar, hurt so good.

1 cup sour cream
3 to 6 tablespoons prepared horseradish
1 tablespoon stone-ground mustard
1 tablespoon honey
Kosher salt and freshly ground black pepper

Mix together the sour cream, horseradish (start with 3 tablespoons and go up from there as desired), mustard, and honey in a medium bowl. Season with salt and pepper to taste. I prefer an ungodly amount of horseradish so that you actually feel it in your uppermost sinuses, making you feel *alive* for a change. It's good to feel alive. Store in an airtight container in the fridge for up to 1 week.

Mushroom and Red Wine Steak Sauce

MAKES ABOUT 1 CUP

4 tablespoons (½ stick) unsalted butter
1 medium shallot, thinly sliced
½ teaspoon red pepper flakes
1½ pounds cremini mushrooms, thinly sliced
Kosher salt and freshly ground black pepper
2 garlic cloves, grated on a Microplane
1 tablespoon minced fresh thyme
½ cup dry red wine, such as Cabernet
    Sauvignon

1. Melt 2 tablespoons of the butter in a large skillet over medium heat. Add the shallot and red pepper flakes and gently sauté until the shallot is soft, about 3 minutes. Add the mushrooms and season with salt and pepper. Cover and cook undisturbed for about 10 minutes, then uncover, give a quick stir, and cook 10 minutes more, stirring occasionally until the mushrooms are golden brown. Add the garlic and thyme and sauté until fragrant.

2. Deglaze the pan with the wine and cook until the alcoholic aroma dissipates, 2 to 3 minutes. Melt the remaining 2 tablespoons butter in the pan and season again to taste.

3. Serve over tenderloin or other steak or on top of your morning muesli or Grape-Nuts. *It's that good, bro.* Leftovers can be stored in an airtight container in the fridge for up to 2 days.

Dry-Brined Herb-Crusted Turkey

MAKES 6 TO 8 SERVINGS

I spent years wet-brining turkey in giant zip-top bags or questionably sanitary beverage coolers. I honestly believe this replicates the magic of true wet brining without requiring full submersion. The muscle is seasoned to the bone, the white and dark meat are as tender as they can be (on account of science), and the skin dries out to ensure a golden-brown crispness every time.

I've been told that a lot of people on the Food Network culinary staff make this bird every year. That alone is the world's best endorsement.

3 tablespoons kosher salt
1 teaspoon granulated garlic
1 teaspoon freshly ground black pepper
1 tablespoon fresh thyme leaves
1 tablespoon fresh rosemary leaves
One 12- to 14-pound turkey
8 tablespoons (1 stick) salted butter, melted
1 recipe Gravy (recipe follows on page 183), for serving

1. Place the salt, granulated garlic, pepper, and herbs in a food processor and pulse until fine and uniform. Rub the inside and outside of the turkey with the spice mixture. Using your fingers, carefully separate the breast skin from the meat and rub the spice mixture directly on the breast meat.

2. Place the turkey on a sheet pan fitted with a wire rack and let it sit uncovered in the fridge for 24 hours.

3. Preheat the oven to 425°F.

4. Fit a roasting pan with a wire V-rack and place the turkey on the rack breast side up. Pour 1 cup water on the roasting rack to catch all those delectable drippings and prevent them from burning. Brush the turkey all over with the butter. Roast for 30 minutes, then reduce the heat to 325°F. The initial high heat will give your turkey incredibly golden skin. Roast for 2 hours, rotating the pan halfway through. The turkey is done when the internal temperature of a thigh reaches 165°F (thighs never lie).

5. Let the turkey rest for at least 30 minutes before carving. Make sure you reserve all the turkey drippings for making gravy. Arrange the turkey on a serving platter and grab the gravy and all the fixin's. Leftovers can be stored in an airtight container in the fridge for up to 2 days.

Now that's how you carve and plate a whole turkey.

Gravy

MAKES ABOUT 4 CUPS

4 tablespoons (½ stick) unsalted butter
5 tablespoons all-purpose flour
4 cups (1 quart) chicken stock, plus more to
   thin
½ cup turkey drippings, strained of solids in a
   fine-mesh strainer, plus more to thin
Kosher salt and freshly ground black pepper,
   as needed

1. In a medium saucepan over medium-low heat, melt the butter until the foaming subsides, about 2 minutes. Add the flour and whisk until smooth. Increase the heat to medium and lightly simmer until golden brown, 5 to 7 minutes.

2. Slowly add the stock while whisking vigorously. Once all the stock is incorporated, add the turkey drippings and simmer for 5 minutes, until slightly thickened. If the gravy is too thick, add more stock or drippings; if it's too thin, simmer for another 5 minutes. Season to taste with salt and pepper if necessary. Depending on the stock and drippings, it may not need any additional salt or pepper. Serve immediately or store in an airtight container in the fridge for up to 3 days.

TIMING IS EVERYTHING FOR THE HOLIDAYS. Many times, people are overambitious and try to execute too many dishes at once. Baked dishes like sweet potatoes, stuffing, and mashed potatoes have a high thermal mass and stay warm for a very long time, so set those out first. Sliced turkey doesn't stay very warm once it's off the bird, so carve the bird while the gravy is still bubblin' away. The hot gravy in the boat is the last thing to be placed on the table. That way, everything is hot. Even if the turkey cools to slightly lukewarm by serving time, it can get drenched in piping hot gravy to warm it right back up.

Pam's Famous Mashed Potatoes

MAKES 6 TO 8 SERVINGS

One snowy, slippery Thanksgiving Day, my brother, Frank James Mauro, was in charge of transporting two pans of my mom's *highly revered* mashed potatoes from the kitchen to the minivan. Like most young men, he insisted on completing this maneuver in one trip (aka the risky yet timesaving One-Trip-Tony Method) . . . and one trip it was: a sloppy trip down the back stairs onto his robust ass, along with my mom's piping hot potatoes. Among the cracked casserole dishes and bloody elbows were gobs and piles of unsalvageable potatoes. My brother claims no one tended to his wounds or triaged his situation. This is true. We all stepped over him and immediately attended to the potatoes. We quickly discovered that no one was getting Pammie's potatoes this year, and it was all Frank's fault. *Booooo, Frank!*

I haven't spoken to my brother in more than twenty-two years.*

5 pounds russet potatoes, peeled and cut into
   1-inch chunks
Kosher salt
6 ounces full-fat cream cheese (about ¾ cup)
8 tablespoons (1 stick) unsalted butter,
   softened, plus more for greasing
1 cup half-and-half, warmed
2 garlic cloves, grated on a Microplane
½ tablespoon freshly ground black pepper
4 tablespoons unsalted butter (½ stick),
   melted
¼ cup minced fresh chives
2 tablespoons minced fresh flat-leaf parsley

1. Place the potatoes and 1 tablespoon salt in a large stockpot and cover with water. Bring to a boil over medium-high heat, then reduce to medium-low and gently simmer until fork tender, about 15 minutes. Drain the potatoes in a colander, then return to the still-warm stockpot to help dry out any excess moisture.

2. In a large bowl, use a hand mixer on medium speed to mix together the cream cheese and softened butter until thoroughly blended, about 2 minutes. Add the mixture to the still-warm potatoes in batches, whipping as you go and alternating with the half-and-half. When the potatoes are smooth, whip in the garlic and pepper. Season with salt to taste.

3. Grease a 9 × 13-inch glass baking dish with butter and scrape the potatoes into the dish. (The potatoes can be covered and refrigerated up to 2 days at this point. Bring them to room temperature before baking.)

4. When ready to bake, top with the melted butter and bake uncovered at 350°F until bubbly and slightly golden, about 45 minutes. Garnish with the chives and parsley.

5. Keep warm in a 200°F oven or tent with foil for up to 2 hours until ready to serve. Leftovers can be stored in an airtight container in the fridge for up to 3 days or wrapped tightly and stored in the freezer for up to 3 months.

....

* *This is a big joke, obviously. My brother, Frank, is the best, and we all make mistakes. And luckily for the family, one phone call was made to my cousin Dave Berni, a chef, who quickly whipped up some stellar—yet not as cream cheesy—mashed potatoes.*

Best. Mashed
taters. Ever.

Minty Asparagus-Citrus Salad

MAKES 4 TO 6 SERVINGS

This is so fresh, fun, and easy that you can't help but make it. The key is blanching the asparagus *hard and fast*, then shocking the bejesus out of it to lock in the color and stop the cooking.

Kosher salt
2 pounds asparagus, trimmed
¼ cup hazelnuts
3 tablespoons apple cider vinegar
2 tablespoons olive oil
1 tablespoon Dijon mustard
1 orange, zested and supremed (see page 140), juice reserved
1 cup canned butter beans or lima beans, drained and rinsed
2 green onions, thinly sliced on the bias
¼ cup minced fresh mint
2 tablespoons minced fresh flat-leaf parsley
Freshly ground black pepper

1. Prepare an ice-water bath in a large bowl.
2. Add 2 tablespoons salt to a large pot of water and bring to a boil over high heat. Add the asparagus and blanch for 3 to 4 minutes. Take one out to test it; it should still have a good amount of snap to it! Drain the asparagus in a colander, then immediately submerge in the prepared ice-water bath to stop the cooking. Let sit for 5 minutes, then drain in a colander. Cut the stems into thirds on the bias.
3. Set a medium skillet over medium heat. Add the hazelnuts and toast until just slightly golden brown, shaking the pan often, about 5 minutes. Set aside to cool, then place in a zip-top bag and crush with a meat mallet, rolling pin, or the bottom of a small skillet.
4. Whisk the vinegar, oil, mustard, orange zest, and reserved juice in a large bowl. Toss with the orange segments, asparagus, beans, hazelnuts, green onions, mint, and parsley. Season to taste with salt and pepper and serve immediately. This is a salad best served fresh.

Aunt Phil's Unstuffed Shells

MAKES 4 TO 6 SERVINGS

My mom has two sisters, and they are both amazing cooks. Aunt Jae (see her legendary garlic dressing on page 191) is more experimental, with a rustic farm-to-table style. Aunt Phil is very traditional and classically Italian-American, serving lots of "rigowt" "manigowt" and basically anything swimming in homemade tomato sauce. Everything they make is equally delicious. Together, the three of them—Pam, Jae, and Phil—can outcook any team of aunts on this fine planet.

Kosher salt
One 12-ounce box medium pasta shells
2 tablespoons olive oil, plus more for greasing
1 pound bulk mild Italian sausage (Mauro Provisions brand preferred)
Two 28-ounce cans San Marzano peeled tomatoes
1 cup whole milk ricotta
1 cup freshly grated Parmigiano-Reggiano (about 4 ounces)
2 cups shredded whole milk mozzarella (about 8 ounces)
1 egg, lightly beaten
One 16-ounce package frozen chopped spinach, thawed and squeezed dry
1 garlic clove, minced
Dash of ground nutmeg
1 teaspoon freshly ground black pepper
6 to 7 slices whole milk mozzarella (about 8 ounces)

1. Preheat the oven to 375°F.
2. Bring a large pot of salted water to a boil over high heat. Add the pasta and cook until al dente according to the package instructions. Drain and set aside.
3. Heat the oil in a 12-inch skillet over medium-high heat. Add the sausage to the pan and brown, breaking it up into large chunks as it cooks, until it's just no longer pink in the center, 10 to 12 minutes. Remove from the skillet and set aside.
4. Place the tomatoes and their juice in a large bowl and, using your hands, crush the tomatoes into chunky pieces. Set aside.
5. Combine the ricotta, Parmigiano-Reggiano, shredded mozzarella, egg, spinach, garlic, nutmeg, 1 teaspoon salt, and the pepper in another large bowl. Mix with a spoon until smooth. Fold in the cooked pasta and set aside.
6. Grease a 3½-quart cast-iron Dutch oven with oil, and spread about a third of the tomatoes across the bottom. Top with about half the pasta mixture and spread it out evenly. Distribute about half the cooked sausage on top. Repeat the process with half the remaining sauce and the rest of the pasta and sausage. Top with the remaining tomato sauce.
7. Bake uncovered for 20 minutes. Top with a layer of fresh mozzarella slices and bake for 10 minutes. If you want bubbly brown cheese, place under the broiler for 2 minutes or so, watching carefully so that it doesn't burn. Let the whole bake cool for a least 10 minutes and serve with a big ol' spoon. Leftovers can be stored in an airtight container in the fridge for up to 2 days.

How'd I do,
Aunt Phil?

How's that oil looking, Aunt Jae?

Aunt Jae's Double-Dressed Creamy Garlic Garden Salad

MAKES 8 SERVINGS

My aunt Jae dictated this original recipe to me and my culinary producer, Lisa, who took the notes. It was a wonderful conversation, filled with a lot of "a bit of dis and dat" and some "throw a little bit of these in, too" and "I don't know, you're the pro, dammit, just mix it and then serve it."

The key is the combination of the super-fortified olive oil, which is the base of the vinaigrette—she calls this the "maranade"—and the pungent, creamy dressing. She makes it for every family party, no matter if we're having BBQ or Sunday Gravy. That salad is on the island and ready to be scraped clean.

Another trick is to dunk hunks of warm Italian bread directly into the "maranade." That's the bee's knees right there.

AUNT JAE'S FRAGRANT VINAIGRETTE "MARANADE"

1 cup extra virgin olive oil
½ cup cherry tomatoes, halved
4 garlic cloves, smashed
Leaves from 2 fresh sprigs of thyme, rosemary, basil—whatever you have on hand
1 shallot, roughly chopped
2 tablespoons red wine vinegar
2 teaspoons dried oregano
1 teaspoon sugar
Kosher salt and freshly ground black pepper

AUNT JAE'S CREAMY GARLIC DRESSING

½ cup sour cream
¾ cup mayonnaise
2 garlic cloves, grated on a Microplane
2 tablespoons white vinegar, plus more as needed
1 tablespoon sugar
¼ cup gorgonzola
Kosher salt and freshly ground black pepper

SALAD

A large bowl of mixed greens, such as romaine, butter lettuce, arugula, and radicchio
¼ cup shaved Parmigiano-Reggiano
1 recipe Homemade Croutons (recipe follows on page 192), for serving

1. To make the vinaigrette, mix together the oil, cherry tomatoes, garlic, fresh herbs, shallot, vinegar, oregano, and sugar in a medium bowl. Season with salt and pepper.

continues

Transfer to a jar or cruet next to the stove if using immediately. This stuff gets more powerful every day, so make a big batch and store in the fridge for up to 3 weeks.

2. To make the dressing, in a medium bowl, whisk the sour cream, mayo, garlic, vinegar, sugar, and cheese until the cheese fuses with the dressing. Season with salt and pepper and adjust with more vinegar if needed.

3. In a large bowl, toss the greens in about 3 tablespoons of the "maranade" so that every bit gets coated in that wonderful oil. Drizzle the garlic dressing over the salad and toss. It will be wonderfully saturated and ready to be topped with parm and a whole boatload of big ol' homemade croutons. Leftovers can be stored in an airtight container in the fridge for up to 1 week.

Homemade Croutons

MAKES ABOUT 3 CUPS

¼ cup olive oil
2 garlic cloves, grated on a Microplane
1 teaspoon kosher salt
½ teaspoon freshly ground black pepper
4 slices white sandwich bread, cut into ½-inch cubes

1. Preheat the oven to 350°F.

2. Whisk the oil, garlic, salt, and pepper in a large bowl. Toss in the cubed bread and stir to coat it in the oil. Then spread it evenly on a large rimmed sheet pan.

3. Bake for 20 minutes, tossing halfway through, until golden brown. Serve warm or cooled or store in an airtight container at room temperature for 1 to 2 days.

Country-Style Radiatori with Vodka Sauce

MAKES 4 TO 6 SERVINGS

My buddy Justin Smith is the best eating partner of all time. Not because of how much or what he chooses to order but because of the quality and timing of these choices: the specific tweaks to the order, the omissions, the add-ins and add-ons. Restaurant meals can be made or broken by the orderer, and Justin . . . is an ordering savant.

Even when we were young and I slept over at his house, our favorite tradition wasn't the late-night mischief, the video games, or pickup games of basketball. It was the pizza delivery. Even at the age of eleven, Justin would order well: one large sausage pizza, well done; one small pepperoni, half cheese, extra pepperoni; and a side of pasta and peas, extra peas. It didn't matter which joint he ordered from—Jim & Pete's, Old World, Armand's—he knew which dish was best at each place, how much to order of each, and what to add on or omit. He micromanaged every order to perfection.

It helped that his father, Richard, and his mother, Val, owned several restaurants all over Chicago (and the rest of the planet). Many of them were Italian, and many of them were dangerously convenient for both Justin and me.

During our teen and young adult years, when we graduated from delivery to dine-in,

he still ordered perfectly. It was never just about being full at the end of the meal; it was about leaving *satiated*—both physically and emotionally. Especially at his own family's establishments, he crushed each order with a deft hand: bread and tapenade, calamari, extra-crispy flat-bread margherita. And always, no matter how much other food was on the way, he ordered country-style rigatoni with radiatore pasta instead of rigatoni.

This beautiful dish was covered in sausage and bright green peas swimming in creamy blush-colored tomato sauce. It was perfect for radiatori. Thanks to Justin's God-given gift, I was introduced at a young age not only to pinkish tomato sauce but also to the magic of radiator-shaped pasta, which provides a glorious network of nooks for the sauce to cling to.

Justin's father, Richard, is now retired, and most of his restaurants are retired as well, but Justin has still got it. We went out to eat over a year ago at a neighborhood restaurant, and I'm still very pleasantly full.

Feel free to add hot Italian sausage crumbles to this. I omitted them because, quite honestly, I use too much sausage in my cooking, and this recipe is just as fantastic without it.

continues

Kosher salt

1 pound fresh radiatore pasta or any pasta that "catches" a lot of sauce

1 tablespoon extra virgin olive oil

1 tablespoon unsalted butter

½ medium yellow onion, minced

1 tablespoon tomato paste

2 garlic cloves, minced

1 teaspoon red pepper flakes

½ teaspoon freshly ground black pepper, plus more to taste

⅓ cup vodka

One 28-ounce can San Marzano crushed tomatoes

½ cup heavy (whipping) cream

1 cup frozen peas

Freshly grated Parmigiano-Reggiano, for garnish

Italian bread, for serving

1. Bring a large pot of salted water to a boil. Add the pasta and cook until al dente according to the package instructions. Drain, cover to keep warm, and set aside.

2. Set a 12-inch skillet over medium heat and add the oil and butter. Melt the butter until the foaming subsides, about 2 minutes. Add the onion and sauté until translucent, about 10 minutes. Add the tomato paste and cook for 1 minute. The mixture will turn a deep red. Add the garlic, red pepper flakes, 1 teaspoon salt, and the pepper and cook for 30 more seconds.

3. Take the pan off the heat and add the vodka to deglaze the pan. Add the crushed tomatoes, return the heat to medium, and simmer until the smell of alcohol subsides, about 8 minutes. Add the cream and season to taste with salt and pepper.

4. Add the peas and the pasta. Toss until the peas are just warmed through but still bright green.

5. Place in a serving bowl, garnish with plenty of cheese, and serve with a crusty hunk of Italian bread. Pasta is best served hot and fresh!

The calm
before the
holiday
blizzard

9

FIRING UP THE PIZZA OVEN

Pizza is my kryptonite. When I'm staring down the barrel of a piping-hot pepperoni pizza, I know the next twenty-three minutes will be a massacre. I eat pizza fast and hard and don't stop until I feel ashamed. I love everything about pizza: the aroma, the initial unveiling as you lift the top of the pizza box, the glossy sheen of slightly greasy melted mozzarella, the charred-around-the-edge pepperoni cups, the hunks of fresh fragrant sausage, and even that first bite that scalds the roof of your mouth and leaves you with skin danglers for the next two days. It's the perfect food, and even when it's bad, it's still good. Luckily, all these pizza recipes are really, really good.

Detroit-Style Pepperoni Pan Pizza

MAKES 4 SERVINGS

My longtime, high-powered Hollywood agent, Jeff Googel, is obsessed with this recipe. He was one of the earliest adopters of this method and sends me videos several times a month of steaming hot bubbling caramelized cheese sizzling in a well-seasoned rectangular pan loaded to the extreme edges with whatever toppings his tummy has a taste for. I'm a pepperoni loyalist, but feel free to top with anything that excites your soul. The crust is so robust that it can handle large quantities of your favorite toppings. The key is to take the cheese all the way to the edge of the dough so it butts up against the inside wall of the pan, trickles down between the crust and the pan during the cook, and forms an ultra-crispy cheese crust around the perimeter. It's so gratifying that I guarantee you, you will eat the crust of each slice first . . . a highly controversial approach.

MOTOR CITY MAD TIP: *Please do not use pregrated cheese for this. Use cubes cut fresh from the block. The anticaking agents in consumer-grade grated cheese hinder proper meltitude and usually yield a less-than-stellar chew. Traditionally, Detroit joints use brick cheese, which is like an American, Jack, and Cheddar hybrid.*

For the best experience, use a 10 × 14-inch Detroit-style pizza pan. A brand called LloydPans makes the standard, most authentic version, and it's available on good ol' Amazon. Have you heard of Amazon? It's a funky little online marketplace that delivers three to twelve boxes

to our house every damn day, which I am in charge of constantly breaking down and storing behind our garbage cans. If not available, use a large square metal cake pan.

3 tablespoons olive oil
1 recipe Detroit-Style Pizza Dough (recipe follows on page 203)
8-ounce pepperoni stick, cut into ⅛-inch slices
2 pounds brick cheese (or whole milk mozzarella), cut into thin slices
1 recipe Pizza Sauce (page 204)
Fresh jalapeño, cut into ¼-inch slices (optional)

1. Adjust an oven rack to the middle position and preheat the oven to 500°F or the highest temperature your oven will go.

2. Grease the pizza pan with the oil.

3. Place the pizza dough in the pan and gently stretch it with your hands until it reaches all four corners of the pan evenly. If the dough is being temperamental, set it aside to relax for 10 minutes and try again.

4. Layer the cheese directly on top of the dough, making sure it reaches the edges of the pan. Spread the pepperoni over the cheese. Layer the jalapeño, if using, over half the pizza for adventurous eaters. Dollop on the sauce in three lengthwise stripes and top with the remaining pepperoni.

5. Bake for 10 minutes, then, using a fish spatula or butter knife, take a gentle peek at the edges and bottom of the crust to make sure they are browning. If the top cheese

continues

My favorite string
instrument!

Cheese it up to the edges.

Three sauce stripes

is browning quicker than the bottom crust, move the pizza to lowest oven rack. If bottom is getting a little too brown, switch the pizza to the top rack. If it all looks good, leave it be. Bake for another 10 minutes, until the crust and top are both golden brown. Using your fish spatula, loosen up the edges and transfer the pizza to a cutting board. Slice into 8 squares and serve! Leftovers can be stored in an airtight container in the fridge for 1 day only.

Detroit-Style Pizza Dough

MAKES DOUGH FOR ONE 10 × 14-INCH DETROIT-STYLE PIZZA

This is a fairly high-hydration dough that is perfect for longer cooks and deep pans. High-hydration doughs soak up all that oil so you get both a spongy interior chew and a crispy exterior. This is great for pan or skillet pizzas as well.

2¼ cups all-purpose flour, plus more as needed
1 teaspoon rapid-rise dry yeast
2 teaspoons kosher salt
1 teaspoon sugar
Olive oil, for oiling the bowl

1. Place the flour, yeast, salt, and sugar in the bowl of a food processor with a metal blade attachment and pulse twice to combine. Add 1 cup warm water, then process for 30 seconds or until a tight ball forms (if a ball does not form, add a bit more flour). Process for another 30 seconds, until the dough ball becomes smoother and then remove the dough. Sprinkle a little flour on a clean work surface and roll the dough with both hands, putting even pressure on it, until it forms into a smooth, tight ball, about 20 seconds. Place the dough ball in a large, lightly oiled bowl and cover tightly with plastic wrap. You can make this dough up to 72 hours ahead. Just refrigerate it in a zip-top bag. Once ready to use, place the dough in a covered bowl before proofing. I'm not a fan of freezing this dough for later use since it's a high-hydration dough. Freezing dough with a high moisture or liquid content will result in a compromised texture when you defrost.

2. Proof in a warm spot for 2 hours, until the dough doubles in size. Once it doubles, punch it down and let it sit in the bowl, covered, for another 15 minutes.

Pizza Sauce

MAKES ABOUT 4 CUPS

This is my go-to pizza sauce that can be used for any style pizza. It's quick and zesty and can be made in a pinch with common pantry staples.

1 tablespoon olive oil

2 garlic cloves, minced

2 teaspoons dried Italian seasoning

One 28-ounce can San Marzano crushed
   tomatoes

1 teaspoon sugar, plus a little extra pinch for
   the angels

Kosher salt and freshly ground black pepper

1. Heat the oil in a medium saucepan over medium heat. Add the garlic and Italian seasoning and sauté until fragrant, about 1 minute; do not let the garlic burn. Add the tomatoes and sugar and season with salt and pepper. Simmer for 30 minutes, until concentrated.

2. Set aside to cool to room temperature. You can make this sauce up to 3 days ahead and store in an airtight container in the fridge.

Napolitano Pizza

MAKES TWO 12-INCH PIZZAS

The first time I ever had wood-fired Naples-style pizza I took a bite and thought to myself, *Oh. Where's the sazeeg? Where's the cheese? I'm still hungry.*

After a couple of slices, I finally got it. This pizza is so subtle and light. The crust is so airy and yeasty. The toppings are perfectly spare, with every bite more harmonious than the one before. I love this style of pizza because it is socially acceptable to eat a whole one by yourself in one sitting.

That being said, I still need at least one and a half of these pizzas to consider myself properly "pizza'd."

DON'T SKIP TIP: *If you have the time, make this dough 72 hours in advance. By letting the dough cold-ferment or proof in the fridge, you slowly develop a ton of yeasty flavor and wonderful light and bubbly structure. It's great with a normal proof, but magic happens when you plan ahead and let it chill for 2 or 3 days. Once you bake your first pizza, you'll be so blown away by how professional it looks that you'll start chargin' yourself and your family for your work as a true red-blooded pizziolo!*

EQUIPMENT: pizza stone or pizza steel and pizza peel

3 cups bread flour, plus more for the work surface

2 teaspoons sugar

½ teaspoon rapid-rise dry yeast

1⅓ cups ice water

1 tablespoon vegetable oil, plus more for the work surface and greasing

1½ teaspoons sea salt

Nonstick cooking spray, for the plastic wrap

1 pound bulk mild Italian sausage (Mauro Provisions brand preferred)

1 cup Pizza Sauce (page 204)

1 tablespoon oil from Homemade Real Giardiniera (page 244) or store-bought hot chili oil

8 ounces whole milk mozzarella, thinly sliced

Fresh basil leaves, for serving

1. Place the flour, sugar, and yeast in the bowl of a food processor fitted with a metal blade and pulse twice to combine. With the machine continually running, slowly add the water through the feed tube. Process until the dough is just combined and no dry flour remains, about 5 more pulses. Let the dough stand for 10 minutes.

2. Add the vegetable oil and salt and process until the dough forms a satiny, sticky ball that clears the sides of the work bowl, 45 to 60 seconds. Remove the dough from the bowl and knead briefly on a lightly oiled countertop until smooth, about 1 minute. Shape the dough into a tight ball and place it in a lightly oiled large bowl. Cover tightly with plastic wrap and refrigerate for at least 24 hours or up to 3 days.

3. One hour before baking the pizzas, adjust an oven rack to the second-highest position, place a pizza stone on the rack, and preheat

continues

the oven to 500°F or the highest temperature your oven will go.

4. Remove the dough from the refrigerator and divide it in half. Shape each half into a smooth, tight ball. Place on a lightly oiled sheet pan, spacing them at least 3 inches apart. Cover loosely with plastic wrap coated with nonstick cooking spray. Let stand for 1 hour in a warm part of your kitchen.

5. Brown the sausage in a large skillet over medium heat until just cooked, about 10 minutes.

6. Coat 1 ball of dough generously with flour and place on a well-floured countertop. Using your fingertips, gently flatten it into an 8-inch disk, leaving 1 inch around the perimeter slightly thicker than the center. Using your hands, gently stretch the disk into a 12-inch round, working along the edges and giving the disk quarter turns as you stretch.

7. Transfer the dough to a well-floured pizza peel and stretch it into a 13-inch round. If you don't own a pizza peel, you can use a well-floured underside of a large sheet pan. Using the back of a spoon or ladle, spread half the pizza sauce (about ½ cup) in a thin layer over the dough, leaving a 1-inch border around the edge. Drizzle the giardiniera oil over the sauce, then layer 1-inch balls of sausage and the cheese on top.

8. Slide the pizza carefully onto the pizza stone or steel and bake until the crust is well browned and the cheese is bubbly and beginning to brown, 10 to 12 minutes, using the peel to rotate the pizza front to back halfway through.

9. Remove the pizza from the oven and place it on a wire rack for 5 minutes before adding a few basil leaves, slicing, and serving. Eat and serve immediately. This style pizza is best enjoyed fresh.

10. Repeat steps 3 through 9 to make the second pizza.

Quick Pepperoni Panzerotti

MAKES 4 PANZEROTTI

During our high school years, Bertolli's River Pizza was my friends' and my go-to weekend late night "snack." We would always call right before closing, when the old man, Frank Bertolli, would answer in an annoyed and rushed Italian accent. "Four pepperoni panzerottis for delivery, please." "Oh Christ-a . . . you got it a-boys . . . thirty minutes."

This always occurred around midnight, and by that time, we had already consumed god knows what, but nothing tasted better than the fresh molten hot panzerottis stuffed into individual cardboard-lined paper bags (yep, bags) after the anticipation of delivery.

We would simultaneously tear open the loose paper to reveal giant pale brown pillows bursting with pepperoni and billowing with

cheese steam. The first bite opened the steam valve, the second bite helped plume the heat outward, and the third and subsequent bites were everything we ever wanted. The trick is to eat panzerottis vertically, starting from the top corner down to the bottom corner. By the end, all that remains is a wedge of crust overflowing with a bubbling hot tide pool of gooey mozzarella, molten sauce, and greasy and spicy pepperoni.

1 recipe Napolitano-style pizza dough (see page 205) or 1 pound store-bought pizza dough
Flour, for the work surface
2 cups freshly shredded whole milk mozzarella (about 8 ounces)
12 ounces pepperoni or sausage or whatever meat your heart desires, precooked and crumbled
½ cup Pizza Sauce (page 204)
1 large egg, whisked, for egg wash

1. Preheat the oven to 375°F.
2. Divide the dough into 4 balls. Roll out each ball into 10-inch rounds on a floured surface. Building in the center of the dough, divide the cheese, pepperoni, and sauce among the rounds. Gently brush some egg wash around the edge of the perimeter and fold over, crimping the edges with a fork and a good ol' pinch.
3. Set the panzerottis on a large sheet pan and bake for 15 minutes, until slightly blond.
4. Let rest for at least 5 minutes, then start eating. Vertically—from one corner to the other—making sure those last bites are nothing but net.

Nothing like the interior view of a piping-hot panzerotti

True Chicago-Style Deep-Dish Pizza (Half Pepperoni / Half Sausage)

MAKES TWO 10-INCH PIZZAS (SEE NOTE FOR A 12-INCH SKILLET/PAN PIZZA)

The polarizing debate over the culinary value of deep-dish pizza and whether or not it's really pizza is second only to the ongoing debate over whether or not a hot dog is a sandwich (see page 259). For now, let's focus on the much-maligned Chicago-style deep-dish pizza, which I believe when properly executed is indeed both a true pizza and a true delicacy. It's a wonderful combination of buttery crust, toothsome cheese, tangy whole tomatoes, and quality meats. I'm done attempting to defend this dish to anyone else in the country. If you've had it right, you'll understand. If you haven't even attempted to try it and still constantly talk crap about it while you sit there in your Upper East Side ivory tower, then I truly feel bad for you. It absolutely is really good pizza.

This recipe is an accurate representation of a Lou Malnati–style deep dish, which is, in my opinion, the best of a very crowded and talented bunch. My go-to order is a medium pepperoni with butter crust, well done, a big ol' Malnati salad, a side of wings, and three ice-cold Peronis out of a frosty mug. That's my birthday order every year, so how could I be wrong?

PROFESSOR JEFF'S TIP: *Do not overwork the dough. This requires a very short knead, which gives the crust its flaky and buttery texture. Just make sure you give the dough a good 6 hours to proof so that it has ample time to develop a wonderful yeasty flavor.*

NOTE: *The recipe for the dough makes 2 perfect medium deep-dish pizzas in 10-inch cake pans. If you are using a larger 12-inch cast-iron skillet, which works well, or a traditional Chicago-style 12-inch deep-dish pan (available on Amazon), use three-quarters of the dough (about 20 ounces), cheese, toppings, and sauce and keep the baking temperature and times the same. The remaining dough can be used to make a fun pan pizza for the kids, such as Bacon and Pineapple Pan Pizza (recipe follows on page 214).*

1⅓ cups warm (about 80°F) water
1 teaspoon granulated sugar
One ¼-ounce packet active dry yeast
3½ cups all-purpose flour
⅛ teaspoon cream of tartar
2 teaspoons fine sea salt
¾ cup corn oil, plus more for oiling the bowl
1 tablespoon unsalted butter, melted
12 ounces deli-sliced whole milk mozzarella
1 pound bulk mild Italian sausage (Mauro Provisions brand preferred)
8 ounces pepperoni, thinly sliced
One 28-ounce can San Marzano whole tomatoes, drained, then crushed by hand
2 tablespoons freshly grated Parmigiano-Reggiano

1. Combine the water, sugar, and yeast in a small bowl. Let the yeast bloom for 15 minutes.
2. Combine the flour, cream of tartar, and salt in the bowl of a stand mixer. Add the

continues

yeast mixture and corn oil. Using a rubber spatula, gently combine until a rough ball is formed. Fit the stand mixer with the dough hook attachment and knead on low speed for 90 seconds.

3. Transfer to a lightly oiled bowl and proof for 6 hours in a warm part of your kitchen. Punch down, then let the dough settle for 15 minutes.

4. Adjust an oven rack to the center position and preheat the oven to 450°F.

5. Coat the bottom and sides of a 10-inch cake pan or traditional Chicago-style pizza pan with melted butter. Place the dough in the pan and, using your hands, stretch and spread the dough out and up the sides of the pan. Make sure the dough is pliable and thin enough to make a dramatic 90-degree angle where the dough meets the wall, so you get a crispy and beautiful deep-dish crust. If you can't get that sharp angle, let the dough rest in the pan, covered, for 10 to 15 minutes to relax, then try again.

6. Cover the entire bottom with the mozzarella, all the way up to the edge. Cover half the pizza with a thin, even layer of the sausage. Cover the other half with the pepperoni. Top with a couple of handfuls of the crushed tomatoes, spreading them out to the edge with your hands. Sprinkle with the grated Parm.

7. Bake for 30 minutes, until golden around the edge, rotating the pan front to back halfway through. Let rest for 5 to 10 minutes in the pan, then either gently lift the whole pizza out of the pan to serve or just cut slices from the pan like a pie!

Bacon and Pineapple Pan Pizza

MAKES ONE 10-INCH PIZZA

4 slices bacon
8 ounces pizza dough (left over from True Chicago-Style Deep-Dish Pizza, page 213, if made with a 12-inch deep dish; see Note on page 213)
1 tablespoon olive oil
½ cup Pizza Sauce (page 204)
10 ounces deli-sliced whole milk mozzarella
4 ounces fresh pineapple, cut into ½-inch cubes

1. Adjust an oven rack to the middle position and preheat the oven to 450°F.

2. Place the bacon in a medium nonstick skillet over medium heat. Sizzle for 5 to 7 minutes, until the bacon is par-cooked and still a bit floppy. Let drain and cool on a paper towel–lined plate, then cut into ½-inch pieces.

3. Add the oil to a clean 10-inch cast-iron skillet and add the dough. Using your fingers, shape and form the dough in the pan to stretch it up the walls. Top with the pizza sauce.

4. Now it's cheese shingling time! Start around the edge of the skillet and hang the slices on its inside wall. Do this around the perimeter of the skillet and then cover the bottom so there is one layer of even cheese slices in the middle. Top with an even layer of bacon, then pineapple.

5. Bake for 15 to 20 minutes, until the top is golden brown and bubbly.

Get that dough up da wall!

Good mozz a must

Half sazeeg, half pepp

Chicago Tavern-Style Thin Crust Pizza

MAKES ONE 16-INCH PIZZA

Chicago-style thin crust is the true favorite of true Chicagoans. It's what we eat every week. Sure, deep dish makes the occasional appearance on our family tables for special occasions or for when you're feeling frisky, but thin crust is our consistent go-to.

It's always crispy, always dotted with little boulders of fresh Italian sausage, and always coated in a layer of stringy whole milk mozzarella.

We also cut the pizza into squares, which makes the eating experience more dynamic. You can have a crusty end piece or a gooey middle piece, or snack on the tiny triangular corner pieces. The fun never ends, and there is something special for everybody. And that, folks, is the reason Chicago is a great city: We cut our thin crust pizza into squares, not gangly, floppy triangles.

EQUIPMENT: 16-inch pizza screen or 16-inch round perforated pan, preferably with a pizza stone, or pizza stone and pizza peel

¼ cup warm water (about 110°F)

½ cup warm skim milk (about 110°F)

¾ teaspoon active dry yeast

½ teaspoon sugar

2 teaspoons corn or vegetable oil, plus more for oiling the bowl

2¼ cups all-purpose flour, plus more for the work surface

½ teaspoon kosher salt

1 cup Pizza Sauce (page 204)

1½ cups freshly shredded whole milk, low-moisture mozzarella

½ pound bulk sweet Italian sausage

1. Combine the water, milk, yeast, and sugar in a small bowl. Lightly whisk and let sit for 5 minutes, until bubbly and the yeast is bloomed. Add the oil.

2. Mix the flour and salt in the bowl of a stand mixer fitted with a dough hook. Set the mixer to medium-low speed and slowly add the yeast mixture until entirely incorporated, scraping down the sides of the bowl to get everything homogenous. Knead on medium-low for 5 minutes, until the dough is glossy and forms a rough ball.

3. Place the dough in a lightly oiled bowl and cover with plastic wrap. Set it in a warm part of the kitchen for 2 hours, until doubled in size.

4. If you have a pizza stone, set it on the bottom oven rack. Preheat the oven to 450°F.

5. On a lightly floured surface, roll out the dough with a rolling pin into a roughly 16-inch round. Set it on a pizza screen (or perforated pan or a pizza peel).

6. Dock the pizza with a fork, poking holes all over the surface to keep it thin and crispy.

7. Working quickly, add the pizza sauce, then half the cheese, then big hunks of raw sausage, then more cheese. Bake until golden and bubbly, directly on the pizza stone, if using, about 15 minutes.

8. Let the pizza rest for 4 or 5 minutes and cut into small squares—never triangles. This is called the party cut. Why? Because no matter what's going on, when you're eating Chicago thin crust, it's always a big ol' party. Serve immediately.

Hunks of sazeeg!

I guess it's clear where
my Chicago baseball
allegiance lies . . .

10

YES, I AM STILL THE SANDWICH KING

The foundation of my career is built on my lifelong love of the sandwich. From my first job slicing meat and making subs at the neighborhood deli to the moment I was crowned "Sandwich King" by Bobby Flay during my journey on season 7 of *Food Network Star* . . . this wonderful life has been fueled by my passion for sandwiches.

The Ten Commandments of Sandwich Creation

1. THOU SHALT ALWAYS TREAT YO' BREAD RIGHT! Butter and griddle your bread whenever possible. This "reactivates" sometimes less-than-fresh bread and also gives it that golden toastiness that everybody loves.

2. THOU SHALT VOW TO KEEP IT SIMPLE. This way, all the flavors and textures can shine through in each harmonious bite.

3. THOU SHALT KEEP IT UN-SLOPPY. The messier the sandwich, the more muddled the flavors get. Too much of too many good things can be a bad thing.

4. COVET THY CHEESE, AND ALWAYS PUT IT ON THE BOTTOM. If the cheese is on top, you *will* get severe slippage, and we don't want half our ingredients shooting across the room. Keep it on the bottom and the sandwich will be more structurally sound. If you're making a grilled cheese or a "melt," then by all mean, load up both the top and bottom. The cheese will fuse to the bread during the heating process, thus preventing any dangerous slippage while promoting dramatic cheese pulls.

5. HONOR YOUR SANDWICH BY CUTTING IT IN HALF! Enjoy the artistic splendor of the beautiful inside layered cross section of your structurally magnificent sandwich.

6. THOU SHALT KEEP IT COLORFUL! The more colors, the more appealing to the eye and satisfying to your nutritional needs . . .

7. THOU SHALT ABIDE BY PROPER RATIOS. Make sure your sandwich is not too bready or too meaty. A good rule of thumb is the 30:30:20:10:10 ratio—30 percent bread, 30 percent protein, 20 percent veggie, 10 percent sauce, and 10 percent more of whatever you crave most.

8. THOU SHALT NOT COVET YOUR NEIGHBOR'S NON-SANDWICH. Enjoy and bask in the fact that you chose to eat a sandwich instead of a platter of chicken and rice like your coworker. Chances are, they are totally jealous of you.

9. THOU SHALT NOT BEAR FALSE MEAT. Use the good stuff as much as possible. Seasonal vegetables, grass-fed beefs, freshly sliced premium deli meats and cheeses, and homemade sauces are the best way to a great sandwich.

10. THOU SHALT EAT AT LEAST ONE SANDWICH A DAY FOR OPTIMUM HEALTH AND HAPPINESS.

Don't tell the other sandwiches, but this was my favorite of the shoot . . . *shhhhh!*

General Tso's Crispy Chicken Sandwiches

MAKES 4 SANDWICHES

I love me some sweet meat. Especially crispy sweet meat. Especially crispy sweet meat at any given American-Chinese takeout joint. No matter how authentic an order I attempt, I always manage to order "a side" of some sort of shiny deep-fried nuggets swimming in a cloyingly sweet yet slightly spicy sauce.

There is a documentary called *The Search for General Tso* about the history of this Americanized Chinese dish. I refuse to watch it for two reasons: (1) I watch TV at night before bed and that is the most dangerous time to get uncontrollable cravings for fried bits of glossy chicken, and (2) I don't want the magic to be ruined by the revelation that while there most definitely was a General Tso during the Qing dynasty, he probably had nothing to do with the invention of this dish.

In my mind, right now, the genesis of this dish is surrounded in adventure and intrigue. It's a majestic story filled with dramatic battles, love lost and love gained, fleets deployed and fortresses breached—all in an attempt to protect the favorite dish of General Tso. Alas, this is not how this dish was created. It was created for people who love sweet meat that verges on a paradox—both saturated and crispy at the same time. I turned it into a sandwich, because who doesn't love a good ol' fried chicken sandwich on a soft bun with crunchy veg and creamy sauce!

4 boneless, skinless chicken thighs
1 recipe General Tso's Sauce (recipe follows)
1 quart peanut oil or vegetable oil
2 large eggs
1 cup buttermilk
½ cup self-rising flour
1½ cups cornstarch
4 tablespoons (½ stick) salted butter, at room temperature, for griddling
4 large sweet rolls (I like King's Hawaiian sweet rolls)
2 tablespoons toasted sesame seeds
1 recipe Asian Napa Slaw (recipe follows)
1 recipe Hot-Mustard Mayo (recipe follows on page 224)

1. Place the chicken thighs in a zip-top bag and pour in ¼ cup of General Tso's Sauce. Let marinate for 3 hours.

2. Heat the oil to 350°F in a large Dutch oven over medium heat.

3. Whisk the eggs and buttermilk in a shallow dish. Combine the flour and cornstarch in another shallow dish. Add 3 tablespoons of the egg-buttermilk mixture to the flour mixture to create some dimension in the breading. This gives you more craggles and crunchy bits. Dunk the chicken in the buttermilk mixture, then dredge it in the buttermilk-enhanced flour mixture. Coat thoroughly and shake off any excess flour.

4. Working in batches, gently place the chicken in the oil and fry on both sides until golden brown and the interior registers at 160°F, 8 to 10 minutes.

5. As always, butter and griddle your bread! Set a large nonstick skillet over medium heat. Schmear butter on both insides of each bun and, working in batches, place butter side down on the skillet. Gently griddle until golden brown, about 5 minutes.

6. To build a sandwich, warm up the remaining ¾ cup General Tso's Sauce in a medium pot and submerge each piece of fried chicken directly into the pot. Let any excess sauce drip off and then place the chicken on the bun. Top it with a nice sprinkle of toasted sesame seeds. Top with the slaw, then drizzle on the hot-mustard sauce. Slice in half, enjoy the colorful view of the cross section, and take a well-deserved bite.

General Tso's Sauce

MAKES 1 CUP

½ cup hoisin sauce
¼ cup rice wine vinegar
3 tablespoons soy sauce
3 tablespoons sugar
2 tablespoons cornstarch
1 tablespoon vegetable oil
2 garlic cloves, minced
2 tablespoons freshly grated peeled ginger
3 to 6 dried whole Szechuan peppers, cut into ¼-inch slices (Found in the international or Asian aisle of the grocery store, these long and lean red peppers give the dish a wonderful numbing sensation.)

NOTE: *If using this sauce for General Tso's Crispy Chicken Sandwiches, make it at least a couple of hours before you assemble the sandwiches.*

1. Whisk the hoisin, vinegar, soy sauce, sugar, and cornstarch in a medium bowl. (Reserve ¼ cup for the marinade if you're making General Tso's Crispy Chicken Sandwiches.)

2. Heat the oil in a medium saucepan over medium-low heat. Add the garlic, ginger, and peppers and sauté until fragrant, about 1 minute. Do not burn. Add the hoisin mixture to the pan, increase the heat to medium, and simmer until the mixture has thickened and the sugar has dissolved, about 10 minutes. Let cool completely to use as a marinade or heat it up to use as a sauce.

Asian Napa Slaw

MAKES 3 CUPS

¼ cup rice vinegar
1 teaspoon toasted sesame oil
2 tablespoons soy sauce
1 tablespoon sugar
1 medium Napa cabbage head, thinly sliced
1 cup shredded carrots (I use preshredded carrots, super easy and tasty)
2 tablespoons thinly sliced green onion
1 Fresno chile, cored, seeded, and julienned
Kosher salt

1. Combine the vinegar, sesame oil, soy sauce, and sugar in a small bowl and stir until the sugar dissolves. Add the cabbage, carrots, green onion, and chile. Toss to combine and season to taste with salt.

2. Set aside in the fridge for at least 30 minutes to let the flavors meld. This dish is best served day of, as the cabbage will unpleasantly wilt over time.

Hot-Mustard Mayo

MAKES ABOUT 1 CUP

Most hot-mustard sauce packets strewn about the bottom of any given bag of Chinese takeout are basically inedible. Too much nose heat and zero flavor. This provides the same gratifying nose heat but with a ton more flavor.

¼ cup boiling water
¼ cup English-style mustard powder (such as Coleman's)

½ cup mayonnaise
1 garlic clove, grated on a Microplane
1 teaspoon honey
½ teaspoon kosher salt

Whisk the boiling water and mustard in a small bowl. Let the mustard bloom in the hot water as it cools completely, about 15 minutes. Mix in the mayo, garlic, honey, and salt. Store in an airtight container in the fridge for up to 1 week.

Deconstructed Eggplant Parmesan Sandwich with Almond Pesto

MAKES 4 SANDWICHES

This sandwich sealed the deal for me when I made it for my final recipe on season 7 of *Food Network Star*. My goal was to show as much technique as possible while reinventing a familiar sandwich. Chef Bobby Flay proclaimed it was the best sandwich he'd ever had.

If you make this recipe while in a good mood, listening to a solid playlist, and enjoying a big glass of chewy red, then you, too, will experience what Bobby did on that day: sandwich nirvana.

Two 28-ounce cans San Marzano whole tomatoes, drained
¼ cup balsamic vinegar
2 tablespoons olive oil
2 tablespoons light brown sugar
Kosher salt
1 large eggplant, peeled and sliced into ½-inch rounds (you'll need at least 8 rounds)
Freshly ground black pepper
1 cup all-purpose flour
4 large eggs, beaten
2 cups panko bread crumbs
1 cup freshly grated Parmigiano-Reggiano (about 4 ounces)
Vegetable oil, for frying
4 tablespoons (½ stick) salted butter, at room temperature, for griddling
4 soft brioche buns
8 ounces burrata cheese, chilled and cut into ¾-inch slices (you'll need 4 slices; it's easier to slice when cold)
4 ounces pickled cherry peppers, drained and sliced ¼ inch thick (about ½ cup)
Almond Pesto (recipe follows on page 227)

1. Preheat the oven to 375°F. Line one sheet pan with a silicone liner or parchment paper and another with a wire rack (if you don't have a rack you can set a colander in the sink).

2. Toss the tomatoes, vinegar, olive oil, brown sugar, and 1 teaspoon salt in a large bowl. Evenly spread the tomatoes on the prepared baking sheet. Roast until slightly caramelized and dried out a bit, 20 to 30 minutes. Set aside.

3. Set the eggplant slices on the wire rack. Sprinkle 1 teaspoon salt over the eggplant slices, flip, then sprinkle another teaspoon salt over the slices. Let the eggplant sit for 15 minutes. This helps remove a lot of the eggplant's water content and ensure a firm and flavorful bite. Pat the eggplant slices dry with paper towels and give each side of the eggplant a good grinding of black pepper.

4. Create a breading line with three separate large shallow bowls. Place the flour in the first bowl and the eggs in the second. Mix together the panko and Parmigiano-Reggiano in the third bowl. Working with one eggplant slice at a time, dredge it in the flour, shaking off any excess. Use your other hand to dip the eggplant in the eggs, coating it completely. Use your dry hand to evenly coat the eggplant

continues

with the panko mixture. Set aside on the wire rack and repeat with the rest of the eggplant.

5. Heat 1 inch of vegetable oil to 350°F in a large cast-iron skillet. Working in small batches, fry the eggplant slices, turning once, until golden brown, 3 to 5 minutes a side. Using tongs, return them to the wire rack, seasoning them with a couple pinches of salt as they come out of the oil.

6. As always, butter and griddle your bread! Set a large nonstick skillet over medium heat. Schmear butter on both insides of each bun and, working in batches, place butter side down on the skillet. Gently griddle until golden brown, about 5 minutes.

7. To build the sandwiches, place a slice of the burrata on each bottom bun, then add 1 or 2 slices of warm eggplant, a couple of roasted tomatoes, a few pickled cherry peppers, and some Almond Pesto. Slice in half to bask in the wonderful cross section of this literally life-changing sandwich.

Almond Pesto

MAKES 1 CUP

1½ cups packed fresh basil leaves
¼ cup grated Romano cheese
¼ cup toasted unsalted almonds
1 garlic clove, roughly chopped
1 teaspoon kosher salt
¼ teaspoon freshly ground black pepper
½ cup extra virgin olive oil

1. In a food processor, process the basil, cheese, almonds, garlic, salt, and pepper until smooth. Scrape down the sides of the bowl with a spatula then, with the motor running, stream in the olive oil. Taste and adjust the seasoning as necessary.

2. The pesto be stored in an airtight container in the fridge for up to 1 day.

Mortadella and Fig Melt

MAKES 4 SANDWICHES

Lorenzo loves mortadella more than any other deli meat. This love started very young and has yet to slow down.

For those unfamiliar with this meat, it's basically bologna with visible hunks of tender fat and the occasional inclusion of pistachios.

This is actually the first recipe I made on the first episode ever of *Sandwich King*. It's simple yet effective, and the combination of buttery mortadella, sweet and crunchy fig spread, and nutty cheese is perfection.

One 10-ounce bag dried figs, stemmed and halved vertically

¾ cup balsamic vinegar

1 teaspoon sugar

8 slices white Italian bread (½-inch slices are ideal if you're slicing it yourself)

8 tablespoons (1 stick) salted butter, at room temperature

2 cups shredded Asiago (about 8 ounces)

1 pound mortadella, very thinly sliced (preferably Boar's Head mortadella with pistachios)

2 ounces pickled cherry peppers, drained and sliced ¼ inch thick (about ¼ cup)

2 cups shredded Fontina (about 8 ounces)

1. To make the fig spread, bring the figs, vinegar, sugar, and 1 cup water to a simmer in a medium saucepan over medium heat. Simmer until the figs rehydrate and the liquid reduces and thickens, about 15 minutes. Set aside to cool slightly for 5 minutes, then place in the bowl of a food processor and puree until smooth, 20 to 30 seconds. You can make this many days in advance. Store in an airtight container in the fridge for up to 1 month.

2. Set a square flat-bottomed 12-inch nonstick griddle pan (not a grill pan) over medium heat.

3. To build the sandwiches, spread butter on the outsides of the bread slices, crust to crust is a must. It may get a bit messy on your cutting board, but I prefer to butter first, build second, so you don't rattle the inside ingredients as you butter. Then, on the inside of each slice, schmear a thin layer of the fig spread. Layer the Asiago, mortadella, peppers, and Fontina on each of 4 slices. Top with the remaining 4 slices of bread, buttered side out.

4. Place the sandwiches on the griddle pan, cover with a lid or large metal bowl, and griddle until golden brown and the cheeses become nice and melted, 4 or 5 minutes a side. Slice and serve immediately with a buttery unoaked Chardonnay.

Mauro's Muffuletta

MAKES 1 GARGANTUAN SANDWICH, TO SERVE 6 TO 8 PEOPLE

Muffulettas are one of the few sandwiches that actually get better with a bit of age. The oil seeps into every crumb of bread, making it saturated and squishy with slick and briny flavor on the inside while still crusty on the outside. The sliced Italian meats become more supple and aromatic when they hit ambient temperature, ensuring a wonderfully smooth bite-down. Everything gets downright funkier as the day moves on, much like the music and overall vibe of New Orleans, the birthplace of this legendary sandwich.

JEFF'S TIP: *This is a great make-ahead party dish that you can knock out the morning of and slice and serve up right before the people descend. Just keep it out at room temperature lightly wrapped in foil, not plastic. Plastic is bad for sandwich wrapping; soft bread will suck up a faint yet off-putting aroma of plastic.*

One 10-inch French boule
1 recipe Olive-Giardiniera Salad (recipe follows)
1 pound aged or sharp provolone, sliced about ⅛ inch thick
1 pound thinly sliced mortadella
1 pound thinly sliced Genoa salami or soppressata
1 pound thinly sliced hot capicola

1. Cut the bread in half horizontally. Spread the salad crust to crust on both cut surfaces of the bread, using *plenty* of its oil. Layer the cheese on the bottom and pile on the mortadella, salami, and capicola. Cover with the top of the bread and let sit for at least 20 minutes so the salad's oil can soak into the bread.
2. Cut into pie-shaped wedges and serve to the masses.

Olive-Giardiniera Salad

MAKES 1 CUP

1 cup pitted green olives
½ cup jarred roasted red peppers, drained
¼ cup capers, drained
½ cup Homemade Real Giardiniera (page 244) with oil or oil-packed store-bought
¼ cup red wine vinegar
1 teaspoon sugar
¼ cup roughly chopped fresh flat-leaf parsley

Place all the ingredients in the bowl of a food processor and pulse eight to ten times, until a coarse "relish" forms. Store in an airtight container in the fridge for up to 1 week.

Chicago Cheesesteak

MAKES 6 SANDWICHES

This is how Chicago does cheesesteaks. Not that it's any better than the amazing Philly cheesesteaks out there! This is just the Chicago version—with good American meat, cooked perfectly, and topped with scratch cheese sauce and crispy giardiniera!

WIZ TIPS: *Use any leftover steak for this: rib eyes, strips, or even big roasts. The key is chilling it in the freezer for about 30 minutes and then shaving it as thinly as possible.*

1 recipe Reverse-Seared Rib Eyes (page 106) or 1 pound leftover cooked steak—see ideas in Wiz Tips
6 sub rolls, hinged or sliced three-quarters of the way through
1 tablespoon olive oil, plus more for brushing the rolls
2 teaspoons garlic salt
1 recipe Easiest Cheese Sauce of All Time (page 42)
1 recipe Caramelized Onions (page 236)
1 recipe Crispy Fried Giardiniera (recipe follows)

1. Freeze the meat for 30 minutes. Using the sharpest knife you have, cut the meat into the thinnest slices possible. The slightly frozen meat helps you achieve paper-thin cuts.

2. Preheat the oven to 350°F. Brush the sub rolls with oil all over the outsides and insides, set them on a sheet pan, and bake for 10 minutes, until lightly toasted.

3. Set a large nonstick skillet over medium-high heat. Add the oil and meat. Season with the garlic salt. Now, don't move the meat. Let it get a nice crispy crust, 3 to 4 minutes. Using tongs, flip the mound of meat to give the top of the pile some heat exposure. Top with multiple ladles of the cheese sauce. Mix it around a bit until the succulent cheese and the crispy meaty bits all marry into one homogenous, nebulous mass.

4. Divide the onions and then the meat among the rolls, stuffing each roll to the brim. Top with fried giardiniera.

Crispy Fried Giardiniera

MAKES 2 CUPS

1 quart vegetable oil, for frying
1 cup rice flour
¼ cup fine cornmeal
1 recipe The Best All-Purpose BBQ Rub (page 35)
1 cup store-bought vinegar-packed giardiniera, drained

1. Add the oil to a medium Dutch oven or medium saucepan and bring it to 375°F over medium heat.

2. Mix together the flour, cornmeal, and BBQ rub in a medium bowl. Dredge the giardiniera in the flour mixture.

3. Working in batches as needed, fry the coated giardiniera until golden brown, 5 to 7 minutes.

Real steak, real cheese,
real crispy pepper . . .
equal a real good
sangwich.

"Serve on the fries!" says Gus. "Keeps the bottom crispy."

The Greatest American Patty Melt in the Country of All Time

MAKES 4 SANDWICHES

This sandwich won me the Best in Show trophy at the 2013 South Beach Wine and Food Festival's illustrious and wildly popular Burger Bash.

My team consisted of me, Chef Darryl Moiles, and his small crew of volunteer cooks from the Four Seasons in Palm Beach (my favorite hotel in the country!). The rest of the crew consisted of my wife, Sarah; brother, Frank; sister-in-law Kelly; cousin Tommy, and his wife, Suzie. Needless to say, we were a ragtag bunch, most of us unfamiliar with the magnitude of the challenge of serving three thousand burgers in four hours on a windy beach.

My goal was to serve up something homey, not fancy. A burger so dear to the Mauro family heart (and hopefully the hearts of the judges) that one bite would call up your happiest memory. Who doesn't love a greasy, gooey patty melt?

We all worked our asses off that evening. At one point, Frank wisely advised me to "double the American." This made the patty melts even more cheesy. Though our offering of a patty melt was controversial (is a patty melt technically a burger?), we won Judges' Choice, in my opinion the most coveted trophy of the night. Everything came together that night. The weather, the family crew, the cooks, the meat, the bread, the onions . . . but what really pushed us over the edge for the trophy was Frank's idea to "double the American." I was told later that what Anne Burrell absolutely loved about the patty melt was the "perfect amount of cheese."

I was fairly new to the Food Network/food festival scene, but that night, with the help of my family and those closest to me, we brought home a trophy and solidified my position in this weird and wonderful world of food stardom.

The next day, Sarah and I boarded the plane home with trophy in hand. The trophy is essentially a retrofitted junior high softball trophy with a burger-shaped chew toy on the top. To me, it felt like my first Oscar—and my first step toward an EGOT.

You know damn well I buckled that beauty in the seat for both takeoff and landing.

1½ pounds ground chuck
1 teaspoon garlic salt
Freshly ground black pepper
8 slices marble rye
16 slices white American cheese
1 recipe Caramelized Onions (recipe follows on page 236)
8 tablespoons (1 stick) unsalted butter, at room temperature
Yellow mustard, for serving

1. Set a large cast-iron skillet over medium-high heat.
2. Form the ground chuck into 4 balls with your hands. Season the top of each ball with half the garlic salt and pepper. Place the seasoned side of each ball directly in the skillet. Using the back of a large spatula, smash each ball to a size just larger than your bread. Season the exposed sides with the remaining garlic salt and pepper. Griddle each side until

continues

the burgers are crusty and darkly seared but medium (about 140°F) to medium-rare (about 130°F) in the interior, 5 to 6 minutes per side.

3. Remove the patties to a plate. Thoroughly wipe the skillet clean and set it over medium-low heat.

4. Place 1 slice of cheese on each of 4 bottom slices of rye, followed by a patty, some onions, and 2 more slices of cheese. Top with the other rye slices. Butter the sandwiches on the outsides of both top and bottom slices (crust to crust is a must). Working in batches as needed, place the sandwiches in the skillet and "dome" them with a large metal bowl or skillet lid to create a proper vortex of heat. Cook for about 5 minutes, or until golden brown, then flip and repeat until the interior is gooey and both sides are golden brown, another 5 minutes. Slice and serve with your favorite yellow mustard as a dipping sauce.

Caramelized Onions

MAKES 1 CUP

2 tablespoons unsalted butter
1 medium yellow onion, sliced thin
2 tablespoons dry sherry
Kosher salt and freshly ground black pepper

In a medium skillet over medium-low heat, melt the butter until the foaming subsides, about 2 minutes. Add the onion slices and cook undisturbed, until the bottoms begin to caramelize, 10 to 15 minutes. Stir only once and cook undisturbed for another 5 minutes. When the onions are the desired golden color, deglaze the pan with the sherry. Season to taste with salt and pepper and set aside.

Greek Tacos

MAKES 4 TACOS

My buddy Matt Lecrone once lied to my face, saying he didn't steal the keys to my car during third period, then proceed to drive my '87 champagne Honda Accord DX to Mickeys, the Greek fast-food joint in our neighborhood. They had great double cheeseburgers called Big Mickeys for ninety-nine cents. They also had a riblet sandwich, as well as big Polish sausage and pizza puffs. And they had the best gyros, especially when you ordered them extra crispy.

If you eat a proper gyro in a car, you can't hide that smell. Not for days, and not without a steam-clean upgrade at the Harlem-Randolph car wash.

That day, I caught Matt in his bold-faced lie because the second I sat in my car after school, I caught one hell of a symphony of scents: onion, garlic, lamb, and yogurt. You can't hide the truth, *Matt.*

LAMB OF TIP: *Double this recipe every time. Eat half, freeze half, and I can guarantee you it will taste even better the next time you eat it.*

1 tablespoon olive oil, plus more for brushing
2 pounds ground lamb
1 teaspoon kosher salt
¼ teaspoon freshly ground black pepper
½ medium red onion, minced
1 teaspoon dried oregano
4 garlic cloves, minced

1 tablespoon tomato paste
2 tablespoons dry red wine, such as Cabernet Sauvignon, or red wine vinegar
4 non-pocket pitas
Feta-Mint Tzatziki (recipe follows on page 239)
Crumbled feta
Tomato-Cucumber Relish (page 103)

1. Heat the oil in a large skillet over medium-high heat. Add the lamb, sprinkle with salt and pepper, and cook until the meat gets nice and golden brown, 10 to 12 minutes. Use a slotted spoon to remove the lamb to a plate. Set aside.

2. Reduce the heat to medium and sauté the onion in the lamb juices until soft, about 5 minutes or until slightly translucent. Add the oregano, garlic, and tomato paste and cook until fragrant, about 1 minute.

3. Deglaze the pan with the wine and scrape up any bits that have adhered to it. Return the lamb to the pan, stir, and sauté until fairly dry and concentrated, about 5 more minutes.

4. Set a square flat-bottomed nonstick griddle pan (not a grill pan) over medium heat. Brush oil on both sides of the pitas, season with kosher salt, and cook until golden brown and bubbly, 3 or 4 minutes per side.

5. To build the sandwiches, schmear the tzatziki on the pitas, add the warm lamb, and top with feta and Tomato-Cucumber Relish.

continues

A Mauro
family favorite

Feta-Mint Tzatziki

MAKES ABOUT 1½ CUPS

1 English cucumber, unpeeled and coarsely grated
1 teaspoon kosher salt
1 cup whole milk Greek yogurt
½ cup crumbled feta cheese
1 garlic clove, minced or pressed
2 tablespoons minced fresh mint

1. Place the cucumber in a fine-mesh strainer or cheesecloth fitted over a medium bowl. Salt the cucumber and let it sit for 10 minutes. Squeeze out any excess moisture.

2. Discard the liquid and place the strained cucumber in the bowl. Add the yogurt, feta, garlic, and mint, mix, and adjust the seasoning to taste. Store in an airtight container for 1 or 2 days. If using after refrigeration, pour off any excess water that may have accumulated on the top.

The Greatest Turkey Sub Ever

MAKES 6 SANDWICHES

It's not a common combination, but this is my non-Italian sub go-to order at any Italian deli. I remember eating this at my dad's office as a kid. New West Realty, on Taylor Street, aka Little Italy. It was directly next door to Conte Di Savoia, a family-run classic Italian deli and market.

I couldn't wait for lunch. I'd walk next door at 10:45 AM and order an Italian sub with fresh mozzarella and sun-dried tomatoes or my favorite: a turkey and provolone sandwich with lettuce, tomato, mustard, and hot giardiniera, best paired with a big bag of BBQ Krunchers! and a cold bottle of root beer.

6 crusty French bread rolls
12 slices (about 8 ounces) sharp provolone cheese
1½ pounds honey-roasted turkey breast, sliced thin
2 Roma tomatoes, cut into ⅛-inch-thick slices
1½ cups finely shredded iceberg lettuce
¼ cup yellow mustard
½ cup Homemade Real Giardiniera (page 244) or oil-packed store-bought (Mauro Provisions brand preferred)

1. If your bread is less than crunchy, preheat the oven to 350°F and toast it for 5 minutes to reinvigorate. Slice the rolls horizontally.
2. To make the sandwiches, layer on the provolone, turkey, tomatoes, and lettuce. Schmear the mustard on the insides of the top slices of bread and top with the hot giardiniera.
3. Wrap the sandwiches in butcher paper and let sit for 5 minutes before eating to achieve that true deli experience. Serve with BBQ kettle chips and a bottle of root beer.

Opa!

11

HAPPY CHICAGO FOOD DAY

Original Chicago food embodies the true spirit of my city: authentic, robust, and full of legend. The late great Anthony Bourdain hit the nail on the head about the spirit of our city and our people and, I'd like to think, our food:

[Chicago] is, also, as I like to point out frequently, one of America's last great NO BULLSHIT zones. Pomposity, pretentiousness, putting on airs of any kind, douchery and lack of a sense of humor will not get you far in Chicago.

—ANTHONY BOURDAIN, MEDIUM

Homemade Real Giardiniera

MAKES 1 QUART

Open up any fridge in the Chicagoland area and you will find at least two or three different bottles of giardiniera. Some hot, some mild.

Giardiniera is also on the table for every meal. It gets spooned onto pizza, pasta, and sandwiches. It's stirred into eggs and frittatas. I believe it's Chicago's greatest contribution to the culinary world.

This is a fermented version, which is how a couple of the manufacturers do it. The lacto-fermentation method gives it that full-bodied flavor and pungent tang that, when combined with the oil, creates magic. Don't skip the soybean oil, it really rounds out all the flavor with an extra bit of funk you don't get with vegetable or olive oil. You can also experiment with the addition of more peppers, garlic, or herbs.

Make sure you sterilize your mason jars in boiling water for 10 minutes and air-dry completely. Prepare the lids by either washing them by hand in soapy water or putting them in a bowl and covering them with boiling water.

EQUIPMENT: four sterilized 1-pint wide-mouth Mason jars or one ½-gallon mason jar with regular or Easy Fermenter lids (for easier gas venting; available on Amazon) and a canner with a rack or a stockpot large enough so water will cover the jars by 2 inches. Optional: Food weights (also available on Amazon) to help keep the veggies fully submerged; in a pinch, you can use several long sticks of celery in a crosshatch shape and wedge them in there to push all the veggies down!

1 tablespoon kosher salt
1 cup ¼-inch-diced carrots
1 cup tiny cauliflower florets
4 to 8 serrano peppers, with seeds, cut into ½-inch slices
1 celery stalk, halved lengthwise and cut into ½-inch slices
1 red bell pepper, cut into 1 × ½-inch strips
2 cups soybean oil

1. Bring 4 cups (1 quart) water to a simmer in a medium saucepan over high heat. Add the salt and stir until dissolved. Let cool completely.

2. Place the vegetables in the sterilized jars. Fill with the cooled salted water to 1 or 2 inches from the top. Make sure all the veggies are submerged with either food weights or celery stalks (see Equipment).

3. Screw on the lids and place the jars in a cool, dry place for 4 or 5 days.

4. Strain and completely dry the veggies in the fridge overnight on a paper towel–lined sheet pan (moisture is the enemy of true oil-packed giardiniera).

5. Resterilize the jars. Once they are completely dry, place the dried veggies back in the jars and add soybean oil until all the veggies are fully submerged. Refrigerate; the giardiniera will continue to ferment in the fridge and get better over time. I find that it's ready to rock after 3 days in the fridge.

Italian Beef, Pot Roast Style

MAKES 6 SANDWICHES

What's to say. This is the recipe that put me on *da map*. My goal was to mimic not only the flavor of a classic Italian beef sandwich but also the texture—without having to invest in a forty-eight-hundred-dollar deli slicer to get that chuck roast shaved nice and thin. The braising and "pulling" process of this meat does that, giving you the tender mouthfeel of a juicy beef sandwich straight from your favorite Italian deli.

Leave it rustic and go with the chunkier pull, or do as my mom does and shred the shit out of it and let it sit in the juice until dinner is served. Pam makes this recipe a lot for family get-togethers. It's simple to double or triple batch, and it holds very well when it's made a day ahead. Quite frankly, Pam makes this recipe better than anybody, even me, but I will never tell her that. At least not to her face. You see, Pam and I have a tumultuous kitchen relationship. From the moment I became a professional chef, we've butted heads in the kitchen. We both think we know better than the other. My formal training versus her lifelong experience cooking for a large immediate and extended family. My technique versus her instinct. My knife skills versus her ability to flawlessly execute that "mom cut"— you know, that thing where your mom picks up a knife and any piece of produce and does that "cut toward your hand with your thumb" maneuver that is questionably safe but works every time.

Truth be told, my mother is the best cook I know, and I love eating her food more than anyone else's. She is the original "Come On Over" queen who always threw one hell of a get-together. Now, don't say nothing to nobody about this, especially little ol' Pamela Louis, but she does indeed make the best beef, so I guess I gotta bite the bullet and tell her to her face . . . "Hey, Ma!"

BEEF TIPS: *Do not neglect the bread. If you can, use Turano original hinged French rolls. They have the perfect structure and protein/gluten development to stand up to the flood of juice. If your bread is not structurally sound, it will fall apart. You can buy the rolls directly from the Turano website or on Amazon. It's worth it. Tell them Jeff sent ya!*

Make sure the sweet peppers are oily, and the same goes for the giardiniera. Don't get the pickled vinegar-packed giardiniera. You want the oil-packed stuff full of pungent and spicy veggies (or make my recipe on the facing page). Make sure to spoon the oil from the jar on top of the beef. You need it glistening.

As you can tell, I'm particular about this recipe. Please, if you're gonna do it, do it right, child . . .

2 tablespoons vegetable oil

One 3½-pound boneless beef chuck eye roast

Kosher salt and freshly ground black pepper

1 medium yellow onion, roughly chopped

1 tablespoon dried Italian seasoning

2 teaspoons red pepper flakes

6 garlic cloves, roughly chopped

continues

Dip it!

This should be
a flag.

½ cup dry red wine, such as Cabernet Sauvignon, or beef stock

5 cups beef stock

2 fresh thyme sprigs

6 soft, hinged hoagie rolls (I like Turano original hinged French rolls)

1 recipe Sweet Peppers (recipe follows)

½ cup Homemade Real Giardiniera (page 244) or oil-packed hot giardiniera (Mauro Provisions brand preferred)

1. Adjust an oven rack to the middle position and preheat the oven to 300°F.

2. Heat the oil in a Dutch oven over medium-high heat. Liberally sprinkle the entire roast with salt and pepper. Brown the roast on all sides until golden and caramelized, 7 or 8 minutes per side. Reduce the heat if the fat begins to smoke. Transfer the roast to a plate and reduce the heat to medium.

3. Add the onion and sauté, stirring occasionally, until just beginning to brown, 8 to 10 minutes. Add the Italian seasoning and red pepper flakes and sauté until fragrant, 1 minute. Add the garlic and sauté until fragrant, about 30 seconds. Deglaze with the wine and cook until reduced by half. Add the stock and thyme and bring to a simmer.

4. Return the roast to the pot with any accumulated juices, place in the oven, and roast uncovered, turning every 30 minutes, until very tender, 3½ to 4 hours.

5. Transfer the roast to a cutting board and tent with foil. Strain the jus through a fine-mesh strainer into a bowl and return it to the pot. Bring to a simmer and adjust the seasoning, if necessary. Keep the jus at a very low simmer over low heat.

6. When the meat has cooled enough to handle, pull it into smaller chunks. Return the meat to the jus and give it a quick toss.

7. To build the sandwiches, place some beef on each roll and top with some sweet peppers and then some hot giardiniera. Quickly dunk the whole sandwich in the hot jus. Wrap the sandwich in parchment for at least a minute to "settle," prep each serving with a small bowl of jus on the side for dipping, and eat away!

Sweet Peppers

MAKES 5 CUPS

4 green bell peppers, cored, seeded, and cut into 1-inch-wide strips

2 tablespoons olive oil

1 teaspoon granulated garlic

Kosher salt and freshly ground black pepper

Preheat the oven to 375°F. On a medium rimmed sheet pan, toss the pepper strips with the olive oil, granulated garlic, and salt and pepper to taste. Roast, stirring halfway through, until soft and lighter in color, about 20 minutes. These can be served hot or at room temperature. Just store in an airtight container in the fridge for up to 3 days.

Garbage Salad with Sweet Italian Vinaigrette

MAKES 4 TO 6 SERVINGS

This salad is inspired by Chicago steakhouse and institution Gene & Georgetti, an eighty-year-old steakhouse under the El tracks where perfect steaks, potatoes, and sides are served to you by career waiters who actually care. Every meal there would begin with a robust garbage salad laden with all sorts of meats, cheeses, and peppers. I have showed some restraint in this version, omitting shrimp, mozzarella, and salami. It's taken me years of health consciousness and fitness to realize salads probably shouldn't give you gout.

FRESH TIP OF THE DAY: *Double or quadruple this dressing and store it in the fridge in an airtight container for up to 3 weeks. It's that good and will be your go-to dressing for every meal, much like it is for my family. Make this your own garbage salad by cutting up and adding any savory leftovers you have in the fridge.*

SALAD

8 ounces diced pancetta

½ head iceberg lettuce, cut into bite-size pieces (about 6 cups)

3 romaine hearts, cut into bite-size pieces (about 8 cups)

¼ head red cabbage, cut into small dice

8 cremini mushrooms, roughly chopped

2 carrots, peeled and cut into small dice

2 Roma tomatoes, cut into small dice

4 ounces blue cheese crumbles (½ cup)

5 to 9 pepperoncini

SWEET ITALIAN VINAIGRETTE

½ cup red wine vinegar

2 tablespoons honey

1 tablespoon chopped fresh flat-leaf parsley

2 tablespoons Liquid Gold Honey-Mustard Sauce (page 116) or your favorite honey mustard

1 teaspoon dried oregano

½ teaspoon chopped fresh thyme

1 garlic clove, grated on a Microplane

¾ cup extra virgin olive oil

Kosher salt and freshly ground black pepper

1. In a medium nonstick skillet over medium heat, cook the pancetta until crispy, 10 to 15 minutes. Remove to a paper towel–lined plate.

2. Toss the iceberg, romaine, cabbage, mushrooms, carrots, tomatoes, and pancetta in a large bowl. Refrigerate until ready to serve.

3. To make the vinaigrette, whisk the vinegar, honey, parsley, mustard sauce, oregano, thyme, and garlic in a medium bowl. While whisking, slowly add the oil. Season with salt and pepper to taste.

4. Pour a healthy amount of dressing over the salad and mix well. Top with the blue cheese crumbles and as many whole pepperoncini as you can handle.

Sausage Pizza Puff

MAKES 12 PUFFS, 1 PUFF PER PERSON IS A PERFECT PORTION

This is a classic Chicago fast-food staple, invented and produced in the city by one company, Il Taco. The only way to describe it is this: If a sausage pizza fell in love with a chimichanga and had a bubbly and deep-fried baby, you would get a pizza puff.

I spent months on this recipe, and the key is the uncooked flour tortillas. They give it the crispy deep-fried blister bubbles on the exterior and the necessary chewy layers on the inside to absorb all the cheese, sauce, and meat.

1 pound bulk hot Italian sausage or hot Italian sausage links, removed from the casings
½ cup Pizza Sauce (page 204) or your favorite pizza sauce
12 *uncooked* 10-inch flour tortillas (available at Costco or Walmart; look for the Tortilla Land brand, which fry up bubbly!)
2 cups shredded whole milk, low-moisture mozzarella cheese (about 8 ounces)
1 quart vegetable or peanut oil, for frying

1. Set a 12-inch nonstick skillet over medium-high heat. Place the sausage in the pan and break it up with a wooden spoon until fine. You want this sausage nice and crumbly, not in large chunks. Cook until golden brown and no longer pink, about 10 minutes. Using a slotted spoon, remove the sausage to a paper towel–lined plate. Let cool completely.
2. Mix the cooled sausage with the pizza sauce in a medium bowl. You do not want this mixture too wet, so go easy—you just want to kiss it with some pizza sauce.

3. Time to fold! (1) Place a tortilla on a work surface. In the upper half of the round, place about 2 tablespoons of cheese, about 2 tablespoons of the sausage mixture, and another tablespoon of cheese. (2) Fold the top quarter of the tortilla down over the sausage and cheese layers. (3) Next, fold the left third to the right and (4) fold the right third over that. (5) Fold the rectangle down so that a short, rounded flap remains on the bottom. (6) Fold the flap up over the packet. Repeat with the rest of the tortillas, cheese, and filling.

Look out, Thomas Kinkade.

4. These can be fried fresh or from frozen. If you are making ahead, freeze them flat on a sheet pan and, once frozen, place in a plastic zip-top bag to store for up to 1 month.
5. Heat the oil to 350°F in a large Dutch oven over medium heat or use a deep fryer. Preheat the oven to 200°F. Working in batches, fry for 6 to 8 minutes if fresh, or about 10 minutes if frozen, until golden brown.
6. Place on a sheet pan fitted with a wire rack and keep warm in the oven.

Vesuvio,
a Chicago
original!

Classic Chicago Chicken Vesuvio

MAKES 6 TO 8 SERVINGS

In the crowded world of Chicago Italian joint chicken dishes, there are always so many to choose from: piccata, marsala, scaloppine al limone, francese, parmigiana, and bocconcini, to name a few staples. And there's usually at least *one* dish named after a real guy . . . like Chicken à la Tony Ocean, Al Pimonte Ford Chicken, or Chicken Uncle Gino. But if you order a Chicken Uncle Gino or any namesake chicken, you're basically getting chicken vesuvio, with additional ingredients like crumbled sausage and maybe some freshly chopped parsley.

That's why chicken vesuvio is king of the chicken mountain. It really is a lovely dish when done right: bright and zesty while still rich and succulent. Like most roasted chicken dishes, it's best when the skin is nicely rendered and crispy with a fair coating of almost-crunchy dried Italian seasoning. The fresh lemon and white wine give the dish a punch of life. The addition of peas is not exactly traditional, but they really tie the room together with their bursts of sweetness.

This dish pairs well with sausage pizza and a big ol' salad!

About 4 pounds skin-on, bone-in chicken
    pieces, patted dry (2 breasts, 2 thighs,
    2 drums, 2 wings)
Kosher salt and freshly ground black pepper
3 tablespoons extra virgin olive oil
1 pound medium russet potatoes, unpeeled,
    cut into wedges about ⅛ of each potato
6 garlic cloves, smashed
1 cup dry white wine, such as Pinot Grigio
2 fresh thyme sprigs
2 fresh oregano sprigs
2 tablespoons Italian seasoning
1 cup frozen peas, thawed
Zest and juice of 1 lemon
¼ cup chopped fresh flat-leaf parsley

1. Preheat the oven to 400°F.
2. Set a large cast-iron skillet over medium heat. Season the chicken liberally with salt and pepper. Working in batches as needed, sear the chicken pieces for 2 to 3 minutes on each side, flipping only once, until golden brown and crispy. Remove the seared chicken to a plate and set aside.
3. Add the olive oil and place the potato wedges cut side down in the hot skillet. Sear until lightly golden, about 6 minutes, then flip and sear the other cut side for 6 minutes. Remove the potatoes to a plate and set aside.
4. Turn off the heat and add the garlic, wine, thyme, and oregano. Whisk and season to taste with salt and pepper.
5. Return the potatoes to the skillet and top with the chicken, skin side up. Sprinkle the Italian seasoning all over the tops of the chicken. Roast the chicken and potatoes in the oven for 35 to 40 minutes, until the chicken reaches an internal temperature of 165°F.
6. Remove from the oven and add the peas, stirring to make sure they get to the bottom of the pan, where they'll heat through. Let the chicken cool for 10 minutes. Pour the lemon juice over the top and top with the zest and parsley.

"Da Mix" Cheddar and Caramel Popcorn

SERVES A CROWD

Some Chicago-based mad scientist figured out a long time ago that if you combine Cheddar popcorn and caramel corn and sell it, people will line up until the end of time to purchase this nontraditional flavor combo. Shout-out to the great Garrett Popcorn and G. H. Cretors for being trailblazers when it comes to rolling the dice with such an outlandish yet successful combo.

Remember, if you or your loved ones lick the cheese-caramel dust off your fingers and dip back into the communal bowl, this is considered a Class 4 DDDD (quad D) offense. Definite Dirty Double Dipping is a highly illegal maneuver and a major misdemeanor in many counties. Therefore, serve in small individual bowls to keep things clean.

Long live Cheddar and caramel popcorn!

2 bags plain microwave popcorn

1¼ cups sugar

⅓ cup light corn syrup

6 tablespoons (¾ stick) unsalted butter

1 teaspoon kosher salt

½ teaspoon baking soda

Nonstick cooking spray

8 cups your favorite Cheddar popcorn (choose Day-Glo orange for that extra curb appeal)

1. Pop the plain popcorn according to the package instructions. Dump out into a large bowl to cool.

2. Bring the sugar, corn syrup, and ½ cup water to a boil in a heavy medium saucepan over medium heat. Cook without stirring for 5 to 8 minutes, until the mixture is a light amber color. Reduce the heat to low and continue to lightly simmer while gently swirling every so often for 2 more minutes, or until a little darker. If the caramel gets too dark, you'll have to start from scratch, so play it safe and keep a close eye on it. You want to aim for 235°F with an instant-read thermometer.

3. Take off the heat and add the butter. Let the caramel bubble as you stir until fully combined. Add the salt and baking soda and stir until uniform.

4. Line a baking sheet with parchment paper and spray with some nonstick cooking spray.

5. Add the hot caramel to the plain popcorn bowl and mix well. *Watch those fingers!* I know you will want to lick that ooey-gooey caramel, but just don't, trust me . . . *don't!* Spread the mixture on the prepared sheet pan and let cool completely.

6. Combine the Cheddar popcorn and the caramel popcorn in a large bowl and watch people's fingers turn dangerously orange as they dive in. Store in an airtight container in the pantry for up to 2 days.

Hot Dog with Fries

MAKES 8 HOT DOGS

It would be cliché of me to start rattling off forty-seven of the fifty reasons that a hot dog consumed in Chicago is better than one eaten in most major cities in the United States of America. I'll just leave the convincing up to number three of fifty: Chicagoans care tremendously about enjoying every bite of *every* hot dog we encounter. When we want a hot dog, we go to a stand that expertly serves a high frequency of hot dogs every day. We don't purchase hot dogs from a streetcar on a street. This is no place to eat a hot dog. Hot dogs are best when enjoyed at a hot dog stand, at a ballpark, or off the trunk of your dad's Oldsmobile.

You see, a lot of these hot dog stands don't have proper seats or tables; just a chest-height counter to lean your big body against while scarfing down multiple orders of dogs and fries.

Picture the Mauro family at our favorite hot dog stand, Gene & Jude's, a legendary seventy-five-year-old establishment serving brilliant Depression era–style Chicago dogs (just peppers, onions, relish, and mustard, wrapped up with a handful of hot, fresh skin-on fries). Since there were usually six of us "dining out," we had trouble finding space for all of us at the counter. So we resorted to eating off the rear trunk of my dad's vehicle, on top of a dedicated towel/tablecloth we dubbed the "mustard towel."

By my twenties, the mustard towel was showing its age. It had years, possibly decades, of mustard stains streaked across its rough white terry cloth and stray granules of salt embedded into its fibers. The mustard towel did have a purpose: It not only kept the mess and oniony smell out of my dad's consistently clean interior, but it was also a novelty, a provocative device that we would love to poke fun at. "Gross, Dad! It's got stains from last year on it!" "Ewwwww . . . it smells, Dad!" "Dad! I can't believe you have a towel in your trunk just for eating hot dogs off the car. Now please pass me one more . . . yeah, with everything . . ."

THE TIP OF THE DOG: *Reason number one of fifty is this: Chicagoans use quality natural-casing hot dogs with that classic snap. They are always nestled in a squishy steamed bun. Whatever your toppings, ketchup or no ketchup, make sure your dog is snappy and your bun is squishy.*

8 hot dogs
8 hot dog buns
1 cup small-diced bread and butter pickles
1 tablespoon finely diced pickled cherry peppers
2 quarts peanut oil, for frying
3 medium russet potatoes, skin on, cut into ¼-inch fries
Kosher salt
Yellow mustard (optional)
1 medium white onion, minced (optional)
Sport peppers (see Note) or other pickled hot peppers (optional)

continues

1. Bring a few inches of water to a simmer in a medium pot. Working in batches, add the hot dogs to a steamer basket and set it in the pot. Cover and steam for 5 to 7 minutes, until the dogs start to darken in color and get super shiny. Add the buns during the last minute or two and steam until properly hydrated and squishy but not wet.

2. Combine the diced pickles and cherry peppers in a small bowl. Set aside.

3. Heat the oil to 350°F in a 5- or 6-quart pot or Dutch oven over medium heat or use a deep fryer. Working in batches, fry the potatoes until golden brown, 8 to 10 minutes. Place on a sheet pan fitted with a wire rack to keep crispy and immediately season with salt.

4. Assemble your hot dogs and top with the pickle relish and any other desired toppings. Plop a big handful of hot fries on top and wrap up each dog in some parchment or deli paper. Let the dogs sit for at least 1 minute to let everything get steamy and delicious. Open and get after it. I keep half the fries on top of the dog as another condiment. Trust me.

NOTE: *Sport peppers are little green pickled peppers packed with a plethora of punch and heat. They are a Chicago hot dog staple.*

IS A HOT DOG A SANDWICH?

A Poem by Jeff Mauro

Are you a sandwich?

Sure, why not?
Or better yet, maybe so
But you're in between some bread!
And I can eat you on the go!

Topped with onions
Peppers
Relish
And varied generous schmears
Of muddled ballpark mustard
And a side of 6 light beers

Served on buns steamed
Into pillowy clouds of wheat
Your natural intestinal casing
Snapping between my teeth

When you're served
wrapped in paper
With piles of skin-on fries
Perfection is achieved
Each new bite a tremendous surprise

But are you a sandwich?
Why must we choose
Who gives a flying frank?
To me, you're not even food

You are as emblematic
as Betsy's fine flag
As Americana
As peanuts in a bag . . .

While watching baseballs fly
Deep, so deep . . . out of bounds
And fighter jets sonic boom
Above sold-out Super Bowl crowds

So, is a hot dog a sandwich?
It's not my place to say
In fact, it's no one's natural born right
To try to make that claim

The discussion must be over
Quite frankly I'm fed up
For a hot dog is perfection
as long as you keep off
the ketchup

My two most
favoritest people

12

Come On Over!

SARAH'S BAKING

If it weren't for Sarah, there would be zero scratch baking going on in the Mauro house. She literally does 100 percent of the baking and is constantly making wonderful things to bring over to other people's homes. She is a natural baker with a great sense of timing, which is ultimately the key to great baking. So take your time with these recipes. Take a moment to enjoy the precision and slow rhythm. Relax. Have some wine. Put on some Grateful Dead and abide by the fact that you cannot rush good baking.

Sarah's Famous Sea Salt Pecan Chocolate Chip Cookies

MAKES 8 JUMBO COOKIES

One thing Sarah learned early on is that every dessert on a table with the Mauro family is for sharing. For a Mauro to order their own dessert is considered highly gluttonous. Mind you, this is after a giant carb-filled meal with few leftovers. I do see the irony here. For some reason, dessert is the daintiest the Mauros ever get. Maybe because we go all in on apps and entrees and salads and table bread? By the time dessert comes around, we show some restraint for once in our lives.

I'll never forget the first time twenty-one-year-old Sarah Jones ordered her first dessert at a dinner with the Mauros. A humble cube of tiramisu was served up, and instantly it was passed 'round the horn like a post double-play sixteen-inch softball until nothing remained but some stray chocolate curls and a sad, thin schmear of mascarpone. The poor child barely got a composed bite.

Needless to say, this turned into quite the spirited discussion later on during our car ride home. She kept saying, "But I ordered the dessert! I didn't eat nearly as much as you guys did for dinner, so I was excited for my own dessert! You guys are maniacs around the dinner table, I mean . . . it really is intense. I can't get a word in edgewise, nobody listens to me [usually this last sentence is uttered by our littlest sister Dana . . . who really is way too often ignored!]. We had a lot of laughs, though . . . Emily—she is something, huh? And that Frank . . . my God, hilarious. Listen, Jeff, I don't think this is gonna work out . . ." Just kidding . . . but only on that last quote.

You see, Sarah comes from the mythical realm of "your own dessert." It's a strange world where the diners order one dessert per person and each plate is cleaned and cleared by one solitary human. Who knows, maybe you offer up a bite, maybe not. Regardless, sharing is not expected.

Not us. Not the Mauro family. Entrées can be voluntarily offered up to the table for a quick taste or bite, but not desserts. Desserts are for sharing.

1¾ cups all-purpose flour
½ teaspoon baking soda
14 tablespoons (1¾ sticks) unsalted butter
½ cup granulated sugar
¾ cup packed dark brown sugar
1 teaspoon kosher salt
2 teaspoons pure vanilla extract
1 large egg
1 large egg yolk
1 cup good-quality semisweet chocolate chunks (I love Guittard)
1 cup pecans, roughly chopped
Flaky sea salt or kosher salt, for garnish
Ice cream and whipped cream, for serving (optional)

1. Preheat the oven to 375°F. Line a sheet pan with parchment paper.
2. Whisk the flour and baking soda in a medium bowl.
3. Let's brown some butter! Place 10 tablespoons (1 stick plus 2 tablespoons)

continues

of the butter in a medium nonstick pan over medium-low heat and swirl constantly, until the butter is melted and the bubbling subsides. The butter will quickly start turning brown; cook, swirling the pan constantly, until it has a dark golden color with a nutty aroma, 5 to 7 minutes, then immediately transfer to a large bowl using a rubber spatula. Add the remaining 4 tablespoons (½ stick) of butter to the hot browned butter to round out the flavor; it will melt quickly.

4. Add the sugars, salt, and vanilla to the butter in the bowl and whisk to combine. Add the egg and egg yolk and whisk vigorously for 30 seconds, until smooth. Add the flour mixture and whisk until no longer lumpy, about 1 minute. Fold in the chocolate chunks and pecans.

5. Use a 4-ounce ice cream scoop or ¼ cup measuring cup to place 8 cookie balls on the prepared sheet pan. I like big ol' cookies, so 8 is great!

6. Top each ball of dough with 2 or 3 pinches of flaky sea salt. You can use kosher salt, but that flaky sea salt just makes these cookies sing.

7. Bake until the cookies are golden brown on the edges but still a bit gooey in the middle, 10 to 15 minutes. Sarah believes underbaking is better than overbaking.

8. Transfer to a rack to cool. Eat warm with ice cream and plenty of whipped cream if desired.

I Can't Believe It's Paleo Chocolate Chip Cookies

MAKES 12 COOKIES

The Food Network fifteen: The inevitable weight gain sustained by new Food Network talent during their first year. Side effects include bigger tummy, puffy cheeks, colorful XXL Robert Graham Shirts, slow movement, acne, irritability, and, in some severe cases, the inability to stop consuming everything presented to you. In some very severe cases (see: J. Mauro), the talent can gain up to thirty-seven pounds.

The dramatic change in lifestyle when I started shooting my first season of *Sandwich King* really did lead me to become my heaviest and least healthy. The travel, the shooting, the dinners and drinks, the festivals—everything adds up. It's all so exciting that it's hard not to indulge in the delicious food and drink that are constantly offered to you. Problem is, I would then have to watch myself on the screen, and I was just unhappy with what I saw.

These cookies coincided with my discovery of the paleo diet and CrossFit, which often go hand in hand. Though my diet and exercise routine is more varied now, the philosophy of paleo eating helped me recalibrate my overall health with a diet of primarily clean proteins and vegetables.

Sarah began making these cookies at the beginning of our healthy journey as a way to satisfy our sweet tooth while still not falling off the rails into a trough of sundae. She is the number one reason we keep this health train on the tracks. She's a helluva motivator and a *brilliant* cook. To quote my very good friend Marc Murphy, she "seasons with authority" and bakes likes a beast. She keeps our food fresh and exciting while still providing us healthy nourishment. It's all about balance.

¼ cup coconut oil
1 large egg, whisked
½ cup coconut sugar
1 teaspoon pure vanilla extract
1 cup almond flour
¼ cup coconut flour
½ teaspoon baking soda
¼ cup (about 2 ounces) dark chocolate, coarsely chopped
Flaky sea salt, for sprinkling

1. Preheat the oven to 350°F. Line a sheet pan with parchment paper.

2. Place the coconut oil in a coffee mug or microwave-safe vessel. Microwave for about 20 seconds, until liquid. Let cool for a couple of minutes.

3. Mix together the egg, cooled coconut oil, coconut sugar, and vanilla in a medium bowl. Add both flours and the baking soda and mix well to form a cohesive dough. Fold in the chocolate chunks.

4. Using a 1-ounce scoop, place cookie mounds 2 inches apart on the prepared sheet pan. Slightly flatten each mound with your palm and top with a nice sprinkle of flaky sea salt.

5. Bake for 10 to 12 minutes, until slightly golden. Let cool completely on a wire rack for about 20 minutes.

6. Since this is a healthier cookie recipe, you can enjoy 4 or 5 of these little protein- and good-fat-filled treats at a time. Store at room temperature, lightly covered, for 1 or 2 days.

Lemon Poppy Seed Bundt Cake with Strawberry-Vanilla Glaze

MAKES 6 TO 8 SERVINGS

Remember how cool lemon poppy seed muffins were? They were everywhere in the early nineties: gas stations, school cafeterias, convenience stores. I thought they were so darn healthy, too. They were muffins, *not* cupcakes. Muffins are permissible breakfast food while cupcakes are naughty desserts. You can eat muffins every day. Daily cupcake consumption can lead you down a dark path. Plus, lemon poppy seed muffins were the *most* healthy muffin because they contained both lemon and seeds. So that's fruit *and* protein.

Therefore, on my way to school, I would often stop by the White Hen convenience store down the block and purchase a giant 940-calorie lemon poppy seed muffin. I'd wash it down with a Diet Rite and proceed to attack the day with an abundance of energy while wearing an ill-fitting sweatshirt dusted in tiny black seeds and lemony crumbs.

Nonstick cooking spray, for the Bundt pan
2½ cups all-purpose flour, plus more for dusting the pan
4 large eggs, at room temperature
3 tablespoons lemon zest (from about 3 lemons)
¾ cup fresh lemon juice (from about 3 lemons)
2 teaspoons limoncello or pure vanilla extract

¼ cup poppy seeds
1 teaspoon kosher salt
½ teaspoon baking soda
1 teaspoon baking powder
1 cup plus 2 tablespoons (2¼ sticks) unsalted butter, at room temperature
Strawberry-Vanilla Glaze (recipe follows)
Yellow and pink sprinkles, for serving

1. Preheat the oven to 350°F. Spray the Bundt pan with nonstick cooking spray, then dust with flour.
2. Whisk the eggs, zest, lemon juice, limoncello, and poppy seeds in a medium bowl.
3. Mix the flour, salt, baking soda, and baking powder in the bowl of a stand mixer with a paddle attachment. With the mixer on low speed, add the butter 1 tablespoon at a time until a pea-size crumble texture is achieved. Increase the speed to medium and slowly stream in the egg-lemon mixture until combined. Increase the speed to medium-high and beat for 2 minutes, until light and fluffy.
4. Pour the batter into the prepared Bundt pan. Smooth out the top and bake for 40 minutes, until a cake tester comes out clean. Let cool for 30 minutes, then turn out onto a cake pedestal.
5. Pour the glaze all over the cake. Top with sprinkles and serve immediately!

Strawberry-Vanilla Glaze

MAKES ABOUT 1 CUP

Zest and juice of 1 lemon
2 tablespoons strawberry preserves

1 teaspoon vanilla bean paste or pure vanilla
extract
1 cup confectioners' sugar

Whisk all the ingredients together until
smooth.

Peanut Butter Parfaits

MAKES 6 PARFAITS

If you haven't played with peanut butter powder yet, I suggest you start immediately. This healthy weeknight "dessert" is ironically inspired by one of Sarah's daily post-workout meals. The magic happens when you mix the yogurt with the peanut butter powder. It basically turns into peanut butter frosting that's actually *good* for you. Add the fresh berries and crunchy peanuts and you've got yourself a quick pantry recipe to either start your day or finish your evening. So serve these parfaits as a healthy-ish fun breakfast or a really quick no-bake dessert.

Do not do as I did and attempt to eat a spoonful of peanut butter powder straight from the jar. It's a very different experience from eating regular peanut butter straight from the jar. You will most definitely inhale it and most definitely choke on a sandy plume of tasty asphyxiant. Come to think of it . . . not a bad way to go.

One 32-ounce container whole milk Greek yogurt
1 cup peanut butter powder (I use PB2)
2 cups fresh blueberries
1 cup dry-roasted, salted peanuts

1. In a medium bowl, whisk the yogurt and peanut butter powder until the powder is dissolved and incorporated.

2. Place about ½ cup of this peanut butter goodness in each of 6 parfait glasses. Sprinkle in about 2 tablespoons of peanuts. Place another ½ cup of the peanut butter mixture on top, then top with ⅓ cup of the blueberries and about 2 tablespoons of peanuts. Serve fairly quickly as the peanuts soften and the blueberries start to get mushy if left sitting for too long. If necessary, you can refrigerate them for about 1 hour before serving.

Oh so elegant!

50 percent pie, 50 percent whipped cream

Atlantic Citrus Beach Pie

MAKES 6 SERVINGS

Custom oyster cracker crust—that's what changes the game here on this easy-to-execute and very bright pie. What separates this pie from its first cousin, Key lime, is the salty edge from the cracker crust, all that fresh lemon, and the generous topping of fresh whipped cream garnished with flaky sea salt.

2 cups oyster crackers
2 tablespoons sugar
8 tablespoons (1 stick) unsalted butter, melted
1 tablespoon lemon zest, plus more for garnish

FILLING
One 14-ounce can sweetened condensed milk
4 large egg yolks
¼ cup fresh lemon juice
¼ cup fresh lime juice
1 recipe Whipped Cream, for serving (recipe follows)
Pink Himalayan sea salt, for garnish

1. Preheat the oven to 350°F.
2. Combine the crackers and sugar in a food processor. Pulse a couple of times, until the mixture resembles the texture of coarse sand. Add the melted butter and lemon zest and pulse until the crumbs look like wet sand, about 30 seconds. Press the crumb mixture into an 8-inch pie pan and chill for 15 minutes.

3. Bake the crust for 15 to 17 minutes, until the edges start to brown.
4. To make the filling, combine the sweetened condensed milk and egg yolks in a medium bowl and beat until the yolks are incorporated. Add the lemon and lime juices and beat for 1 to 2 minutes, until smooth. Pour into the prepared pie shell (the pie shell can still be warm).
5. Bake for 15 to 18 minutes, until the filling has set. Let cool to room temperature, then chill in the refrigerator for at least 2 hours. This pie can be made a day in advance—just wait to top with the whipped cream until right before serving.
6. Top with an overabundance of whipped cream, pink Himalayan sea salt, and lemon zest.

Whipped Cream

MAKES ABOUT 4 CUPS

2 cups (1 pint) heavy (whipping) cream
¼ cup sugar
Couple pinches of sea salt
1 teaspoon vanilla bean paste or pure vanilla extract

Combine the cream, sugar, salt, and vanilla bean paste in a medium cold bowl. Beat to medium-stiff peaks.

Cookie Butter Pie

MAKES 6 TO 8 SERVINGS

This is like eating a pie entirely made out of cookies. Not like a cookie dough pie or cookies and cream pie, in which there are just a couple of bits of cookie crumbles inside the pie and a couple of decorative cookie garnishes on the top. This pie is basically 90 percent cookie. Should I go on . . . ?

SWEET TIP: *Pipe on the whipped cream right before you serve it. Not only will the whipped cream be super fresh and airy, but people love to watch the piping process.*

CRUST
Nonstick cooking spray, for the pie plate
10 ounces packaged gingersnap cookies
¼ cup packed light brown sugar
6 tablespoons (¾ stick) unsalted butter, melted

PIE FILLING
2 cups (1 pint) heavy (whipping) cream
¾ cup confectioners' sugar
1 tablespoon vanilla bean paste or pure vanilla extract
One 8-ounce package full-fat cream cheese, at room temperature
1 cup cookie butter (I like Trader Joe's)
½ teaspoon orange extract
¼ cup salted cashews, finely chopped, for garnish
1 tablespoon orange zest, for garnish (optional)

1. Preheat the oven to 350°F. Spray a 9-inch pie plate with nonstick cooking spray.

2. To make the crust, place the cookies and brown sugar in the bowl of a food processor. Pulse into fine crumbs. Add the melted butter and pulse a couple of more times, until the mixture resembles wet sand. Press the mixture firmly into the prepared pie plate, going up the sides.

3. Bake for 7 to 8 minutes, until golden. Let cool completely before filling.

4. To make the filling, combine the cream, confectioners' sugar, and vanilla bean paste in the clean, cold bowl of a stand mixer. Beat into stiff peaks on medium-high speed. Gently scoop half the whipped cream into a pastry bag fitted with a ½-inch star tip and refrigerate. If you don't have that equipment, you can use a zip-top bag and just cut off a small section of one of the corners to create a makeshift pastry bag.

5. Scoop the other half of the whipped cream into a clean bowl. In the bowl of the stand mixer (no need to clean!), beat the cream cheese on medium speed for 1 minute, until light and fluffy. Add the cookie butter and orange extract and beat until light and fluffy, about 3 minutes.

6. Gently fold in the whipped cream from the other bowl. Do not overmix. Pour the mixture into the cooled pie crust and refrigerate for 2 hours, until set. You can make the pie a day ahead. Just wait until right before serving to top it with the piped whipped cream.

7. Using the whipped cream reserved in the pastry bag, decorate the top of the pie with small star mounds around its perimeter. Garnish with the cashews and, if desired, orange zest.

Totally unplanned and
random reveal of the word
"pie" for this first slice

School of Rock
concert T from
one of Lorenzo's
summer concerts

Gus's Pantry Raid Milkshake

As mentioned in the breakfast chapter, Gus made only three things for us kids: frittatas, hash browns, and milkshakes. The milkshakes were few and far between, but when he fired up the blender, we knew we were getting a proper pantry-raiding milkshake. In fact, there was so much cereal matter, granola, and cookie particles in the shake, it would be impervious to melting and just remain solid for an hour. It was the strangest thing: crunchy, creamy, sweet, and *eventually* slurp-able.

1 cup whole milk, plus more to thin
1 pint vanilla ice cream, ideally softened at room temperature for 30 minutes or, in a pinch, microwaved in 15-second increments until softened a bit
1 super-ripe banana
2 tablespoons smooth peanut butter
1 cup total of any of the following:
    Granola
    Honey Bunches of Oats
    Golden Grahams
    Leftover chocolate-based Halloween candy
    Cookies from your child's lunchbox
Canned whipped cream, for garnish
Maraschino cherries, for garnish

1. Add the milk to the blender first to create a blendable "quicksand" for the ice cream and other additions. Add the ice cream, banana, and peanut butter and blend until smooth, 10 to 15 seconds. You may need to add more milk if your mixture is too thick. Add about ¼ cup at a time until things get going.

2. To take your shake to the next level, start adding all your favorite pantry pulls. Pulse until the shake is uniform but your mix-ins still retain a little chunk.

3. Pour into pint glasses and top with some canned whipped cream and a cherry.

Deconstructed Cannoli Chips and Dip

MAKES 6 TO 8 SERVINGS

The minute a crispy cannoli shell is filled with rich ricotta, it starts to degrade at a rapid pace. It takes less than a half hour for the whole experience to become compromised. By the time you get home, the bakery box is a mess of fallen pistachio crumbles, weeping ricotta, and, often, soggy shells.

This dip is a wonderful and beyond simple way to replicate, over and over, that perfect first bite of a cannoli when you inhale a plume of confectioners' sugar as your teeth start to crunch down on the bubbly shell and the textures of the pistachio and chocolate chips swim together in your mouth in a sea of creamy and sweet ricotta filling. It's my favorite first bite in the pastry world . . .

Then you go in for the second bite . . . and all bets are off. Shards of shell fall around you like confetti in a Fellini film. Your fancy new button-down is coated in confectioners' sugar while a stray maraschino ricochets off your husky Bugle Boys and rolls across the linoleum floor. You try to catch all the falling bits, but you're too worried about chewing and tasting and getting all that wonderful flavor into your mouth!

By the time you finish your second bite of cannoli, your shirt looks like a dessert table at the end of your cousin's wedding and your floor is beyond repair. And God forbid you have to share a cannoli with others and you attempt to cut it up "for the table" . . . *madone!* Might as well break out the Shop-Vac and get a divorce attorney on the horn.

Do yourself and your family a favor by making this inventive and easy-to-make cannoli dip instead.

Canola oil, for frying
One 36-count package square wonton wrappers, cut in half diagonally
2 cups whole milk ricotta
½ cup confectioners' sugar, plus more for dusting
3 tablespoons orange liqueur, such as Grand Marnier
1 cup heavy (whipping) cream
1 cup chocolate chips
½ cup pistachios, coarsely chopped
½ cup maraschino cherries, chopped
Zest of 1 orange

1. Fill a Dutch oven one-third full of oil and heat it to 350°F over medium heat. Set a wire rack on a rimmed sheet pan.

2. Fry the wonton wrappers, working in batches so they fit in a single layer. Flip once or twice until golden brown, 4 to 5 minutes. Remove with tongs or a slotted spoon and drain on the prepared wire rack.

3. Combine the ricotta, sugar, and liqueur in a large bowl and stir until well mixed. Using a handheld mixer, whip the cream in a separate bowl until soft peaks form. Gently fold the whipped cream and ½ cup of the chocolate chips into the ricotta mixture.

4. Transfer the ricotta-cream mixture to a medium dip bowl or 8 × 8-inch baking dish and spread it out evenly. Starting from the left side, make a row of the pistachios, then the cherries, then the remaining ½ cup chocolate chips. Sprinkle the top with the orange zest. Dust the wonton chips with confectioners' sugar and serve on the side.

Acknowledgments

First off, I need to say that this book was birthed on the eve of one of the most trying and difficult times on our planet. We started principal photography and styling for it the week before the entire country was first quarantined because of the COVID-19 pandemic. The day we finished photography was the day before NYC, Chicago, and LA were issued stay-at-home orders. The impending doom was palpable and raw all week. The stress of the uncertain future was hard to process. My photographer, Ken, and culinary lead, Tim, are based on the East Coast and were far away from their wives and children.

We hunkered down in our little Airbnb in historic Oak Park, Illinois, right down the block from both my high school and my favorite beef stand. We worked endlessly and furiously. Our unspoken motivation: getting this book finished before the world collapsed. And by God, we did it.

As I write this four months later, most of the country is still in quarantine or just starting to open up. The last dinner out I had was our book team's wrap dinner at our favorite Mexican joint, Maria's, on Harlem. We ate giant shells filled with chorizo-laden queso fundido and drank way too many strong premium margaritas. We had so many laughs that night. We "birthday'd" Tim Macklin even though it wasn't his birthday (free shot and a song!), we stuffed our gullets with asada, and we toasted to the possible end of the world.

Today. The world is still chugging along and people are cooking in their kitchens now more than ever. Hopefully, even by the time you read this, we are back to normal.

THANK YOUSE GUYS

First of all, many thanks to my editor, Cassie Jones, for taking that first meeting and eventually creating a home for my first cookbook, which was a long time coming. Thank you for your expertise and creativity throughout this journey. I've learned so much. Thank you as well to Jill Zimmerman for your fine-tooth comb and guidance. Cannot wait to do another one! Wait, did I just say that out loud . . . To Ken Goodman, photographer to the stars: Your reputation is the best in the business for a reason—you're the goddamn best in the business. You're fluent in the languages of both chefs and entertainers. You have a brilliant eye and a boundless work ethic. Thank you for coming on board and joining our small yet *robust* cookbook crew. Until next time . . .

Lisa Krych, my right-hand maestro who not only helped me and tested many of the recipes in this book but also kept me on track and organized the entire way: You are a brilliant cook, a gifted stylist, and a wonderful manager of all things. You're a partner for life. Thank you, too, to Lisa's wife, J, for helping out with the setup at the house and for lending us Lisa for so long.

To Big Timmy Macklin slumming with us in Chicago, your hustle and precision in that tiny Airbnb kitchen kept us 100 percent on schedule and out of the weeds. You're a joy to be around on set of *The Kitchen* and even more so during our photoshoot. You're a friend for life. A Baba Booey to you.

Thank you to Mak and John and their wonderful family for hosting us. If you ever need a fabulous Airbnb in Oak Park, right in the heart of Frank Lloyd Wright land and right next to the city, look them up. The address is 921 Chicago Ave., Oak Park, IL.

Special shout-out to Snake River Farms and David Yasuda in Idaho for providing me and the gang with the country's best beef and pork. That there Tomahawk on the cover is my favorite piece of beef on the planet. Thanks for continued generosity.

To my literary agents, Eve Atterman and Andy McNicol, for cannonballing immediately into the deep end of this project and making sure we found the right home for this book.

To my high-powered Hollywood agents, Jeff Googel, Josh Bider, and Strand Conover, for making those first meetings happen and continuing to be the best agents a little boy would ever need.

Big additional thanks to Jeff Googel for naming this book, not because it was just a clever title but because he knows me *well* and knew it made perfect sense. You're the best in the business, brother.

To my cohosts on *The Kitchen*: Geoffrey, Sunny, Alex, and Katie. We are not cohosts, we are family. May we work together forever and ever and ever. I love you guys. To the Murphy family: Marc, Pam, Gabrielle, Emily, Jeff and John, Campbell, and Callen. Thanks for being our first and closest Food Network Friends and sharing your homes and lives with Sarah and me. To the entire crew at Food Network, including Irika Slavin and Lauren Mueller, for your guidance since literally *day one*. To the entire team running the FN Empire: Seth, Sklar, Courtney White, Lynn Sadofski, Karen Berrios, Neil Regan, and Jen Quainton and to the BSTV crew: Beth Burke and Blake Swerdloff, Candice Lombardi, Christine Cardona, Maggie Barnes, and Elias Holtz.

Thanks to all our bestest friends and neighbors. Brian, Erin, and Brady Hahn, for being amazing friends and for lending me that legitimate yellow analog phone for the cover shoot. Thanks to our neighbors, the Martins, Nelsons, Natales, DuBois, Heinzs, Stierwalts, and Johnsons. Big shout-out to Terry and Terry Roache next door and their tiny little boy, Paul. Thanks for eating all our leftovers and keeping food waste to a minimum.

Thank you to my boys from the neighborhood, Matt Lecrone, Niles Townsend, David Winski, and the entire O'Connor clan for their support over the years. Thanks to my Irish consiglieri, Neil, and Heather, Dean, and Eamon. Also, our very good friend Tom Zimmerman passed away while writing this book. He was a brilliant brain, a talented songwriter, and a great friend. You are missed by all of us, Tom. To experience some of Tom's musical brilliance, check out his bands, Tommy Slax and The Interociter, on Spotify.

Thanks to Deanna Abbinanti and the entire Abbinanti family (Gia, Iggy, Andrea, Mike, Rocco, Cassie, Bobby, Linda) and all Sarah's lady friends for keeping her laughing (Jackie, Lisa, April, Tammy, Teresa, and Holly).

To my extended family, who were the reason and influence behind this book: Aunt Catherine Mauro, Aunt Fran Mauro, Uncle Nick Speziale and Aunt Phil Speziale, Uncle Neil Renzi, Uncle Dave Berni, Aunt Jae Berni, Nick and Liz Speziale, Gina and Tom Taylor, Christen and Mike Rice, Jessica and Mike Degen, David Berni, Jenny Berni and Uncle Tim, Alison and Marc Gaddis, Joe and Joellen Berni, Danny and Annie Berni, and Melissa Renzi and Jason. Huge thanks to my California cousin Joe Ballarini, who fifteen years ago urged me to move to LA to begin pursuing a career in food TV. You believed in me and were instrumental in forging the foundation of my crazy career. Love you, Kara, Owen, and Elodie. Shout-out to my boy Ali Khan (and Brearly and Healthy!), who was my culinary partner in crime during the beginning with Chef Jeff and Ali Days. So glad you made it on the network, brother. We did it.

To my siblings, Frank, Emily, and Dana, as well as my sister-in-law, Kelly Mauro, and my two nephews, Frankie and Leno Mauro: May we forever continue to laugh together, cry together, bust each other's balls to keep us all humble. I love you all very much.

To my in-laws, Alice Marjorie Ross and James Paul Jones: I couldn't imagine having better in-laws. You fully believed in me and supported our relationship since the first time we met in June of 2000. You've housed us a half a dozen times over the years and always watch our dogs and child any time we ask. I love you guys very much. Big hug to the whole Jones/Ross crew: Auntie Margaret Ross and Sufian, Uncle Garland and Debbie, Chloe, J.R., Uncle Frank, Jan and Rochelle, and Cheryl.

To my mom and dad, Pam and Gus: Never once did you discourage my talents or passions. Never once did you encourage a responsible "fallback plan." You always supported my crazy endeavors, showed up to my comedy shows, school plays, and delis and restaurants. Thank you for birthing me, raising me, and showing me how to be a great parent, sibling, and spouse.

To my son, Lorenzo Lucca Mauro: I love you more than anything. You're a great sport and consistently roll with all the punches thrown at you. You hate photoshoots just as much as I do, but you always remained professional and still managed to have fun. You're going to grow up and do great things.

To my wife and stunning partner of over two decades, Sarah Edith Mauro (née Jones): Without you, none of this would be possible. I would have procrastinated until the end of time while slowly coming apart at the seams. This book was a bear and you were the mama bear of us all. Especially during the hectic beginning of the COVID-19 pandemic when the country was flooding the grocery stores, hoarding wipes and toilet paper. You showed no fear, masked up, and shopped multiple times a day to purchase food for this cookbook. I'll love you forever.

Universal Conversion Chart

OVEN TEMPERATURE EQUIVALENTS

250°F = 120°C
275°F = 135°C
300°F = 150°C
325°F = 160°C
350°F = 180°C
375°F = 190°C
400°F = 200°C
425°F = 220°C
450°F = 230°C
475°F = 240°C
500°F = 260°C

MEASUREMENT EQUIVALENTS

Measurements should always be level unless directed otherwise.

⅛ teaspoon = 0.5 mL
¼ teaspoon = 1 mL
½ teaspoon = 2 mL
1 teaspoon = 5 mL
1 tablespoon = 3 teaspoons = ½ fluid ounce = 15 mL
2 tablespoons = ⅛ cup = 1 fluid ounce = 30 mL
4 tablespoons = ¼ cup = 2 fluid ounces = 60 mL
5⅓ tablespoons = ⅓ cup = 3 fluid ounces = 80 mL
8 tablespoons = ½ cup = 4 fluid ounces = 120 mL
10⅔ tablespoons = ⅔ cup = 5 fluid ounces = 160 mL
12 tablespoons = ¾ cup = 6 fluid ounces = 180 mL
16 tablespoons = 1 cup = 8 fluid ounces = 240 mL

Index

Note: Page references in *italics* indicate photographs.

Sarah's List:

- plan your lighting - soft lighting is best

- make your centerpieces

- plan a cooking schedule

- coffee - our family LOVES strong coffee

- extra toilet paper :)

- have all platters and serving pieces you will need